MASTER THE™ DSST®

Principles of Public Speaking Exam

About Peterson's

Peterson's® has been your trusted educational publisher for more than 50 years. It's a milestone we're quite proud of, as we continue to offer the most accurate, dependable, high-quality educational content in the field, providing you with everything you need to succeed. No matter where you are on your academic or professional path, you can rely on Peterson's for our books, online information, expert test-prep tools, the most up-to-date education exploration data, and the highest quality career success resources—everything you need to achieve your education goals. For our complete line of products, visit **www.petersons.com.**

For more information, contact Peterson's, 4380 S. Syracuse Street, Suite 200, Denver CO 80237; 800-338-3282 Ext. 54229; or visit us online at **www.petersons.com.**

© 2022 Peterson's

ISBN-13: 978-0-7689-4470-9

Printed in the United States of America

10 9 8 7 6 5 4 3 2 1   24 23 22

Contents

Before You Begin

HOW THIS BOOK IS ORGANIZED

Peterson's *Master the*™ *DSST*® *Principles of Public Speaking Exam* provides a diagnostic test, subject-matter review, and a post-test.

- **Diagnostic Test**—Twenty multiple-choice questions, followed by an answer key with detailed answer explanations
- **Assessment Grid**—A chart designed to help you identify areas that you need to focus on based on your test results
- **Subject-Matter Review**—General overview of the exam subject, followed by a review of the relevant topics and terminology covered on the exam
- **Post-test**—Sixty multiple-choice questions, followed by an answer key and detailed answer explanations

The purpose of the diagnostic test is to help you figure out what you know—or don't know. The twenty multiple-choice questions are similar to the ones found on the DSST exam, and they should provide you with a good idea of what to expect. Once you take the diagnostic test, check your answers to see how you did. Included with each correct answer is a brief explanation regarding why a specific answer is correct, and in many cases, why other options are incorrect. Use the assessment grid to identify the questions you miss so that you can spend more time reviewing that information later. As with any exam, knowing your weak spots greatly improves your chances of success.

Following the diagnostic test is a subject-matter review. The review summarizes the various topics covered on the DSST exam. Key terms are defined; important concepts are explained; and when appropriate, examples are provided. As you read the review, some of the information may seem familiar while other information may seem foreign. Again, take note of the unfamiliar because that will most likely cause you problems on the actual exam.

OTHER DSST® PRODUCTS BY PETERSON'S

Books, flashcards, practice tests, and videos available online at
www.petersons.com/testprep/dsst

- A History of the Vietnam War
- Art of the Western World
- Astronomy
- Business Mathematics
- Business Ethics and Society
- Civil War and Reconstruction
- Computing and Information Technology
- Criminal Justice
- Environmental Science
- Ethics in America
- Ethics in Technology
- Foundations of Education
- Fundamentals of College Algebra
- Fundamentals of Counseling
- Fundamentals of Cybersecurity
- General Anthropology
- Health and Human Development
- History of the Soviet Union
- Human Resource Management
- Introduction to Business
- Introduction to Geography
- Introduction to Geology
- Introduction to Law Enforcement
- Introduction to World Religions
- Lifespan Developmental Psychology
- Math for Liberal Arts
- Management Information Systems
- Money and Banking
- Organizational Behavior
- Personal Finance
- Principles of Advanced English Composition
- Principles of Finance
- Principles of Public Speaking
- Principles of Statistics
- Principles of Supervision
- Substance Abuse
- Technical Writing

Like what you see? Get unlimited access to Peterson's full catalog of DSST practice tests, instructional videos, flashcards, and more at **www.petersons.com/testprep/dsst.**

Chapter 1

All About the DSST® Exam

WHAT IS DSST®?

Previously known as the DANTES Subject Standardized Tests, the DSST program provides the opportunity for individuals to earn college credit for what they have learned outside of the traditional classroom. Accepted or administered at more than 1,500 colleges and universities nationwide and approved by the American Council on Education (ACE), the DSST program enables individuals to use the knowledge they have acquired outside the classroom to accomplish their educational and professional goals.

WHY TAKE A DSST® EXAM?

DSST exams offer a way for you to save both time and money in your quest for a college education. Why enroll in a college course in a subject you already understand? For more than 30 years, the DSST program has offered the perfect solution for individuals who are knowledgeable in a specific subject and want to save both time and money. A passing score on a DSST exam provides physical evidence to universities of proficiency in a specific subject. More than 1,500 accredited and respected colleges and universities across the nation award undergraduate credit for passing scores on DSST exams. With the DSST program, individuals can shave months off the time it takes to earn a degree.

The DSST program offers numerous advantages for individuals in all stages of their educational development:

- Adult learners
- College students
- Military personnel

Adult learners desiring college degrees face unique circumstances—demanding work schedules, family responsibilities, and tight budgets. Yet adult learners also have years of valuable work experience that can be applied toward a degree through the DSST program. For example, adult learners with on-the-job experience in business and management might be able to skip the Business 101 courses if they earn passing marks on DSST exams such as Introduction to Business and Principles of Supervision.

Adult learners can put their prior learning into action and move forward with more advanced course work. Adults who have never enrolled in a college course may feel a little uncertain about their abilities. If this describes your situation, then sign up for a DSST exam and see how you do. A passing score may be the boost you need to realize your dream of earning a degree. With family and work commitments, adult learners often feel they lack the time to attend college. The DSST program provides adult learners with the unique opportunity to work toward college degrees without the time constraints of semester-long course work. DSST exams take two hours or less to complete. In one weekend, you could earn credit for multiple college courses.

The DSST exams also benefit students who are already enrolled in a college or university. With college tuition costs on the rise, most students face financial challenges. The fee for each DSST exam starts at $100 (plus administration fees charged by some testing facilities)—significantly less than the $750 average cost of a 3-hour college class. Maximize tuition assistance by taking DSST exams for introductory or mandatory course work. Once you earn a passing score on a DSST exam, you are free to move on to higher-level course work in that subject matter, take desired electives, or focus on courses in a chosen major.

Not only do college students and adult learners profit from DSST exams, but military personnel reap the benefits as well. If you are a member of the armed services at home or abroad, you can initiate your post-military career by taking DSST exams in areas with which you have experience. Military personnel can gain credit anywhere in the world, thanks to the fact that almost all of the tests are available through the internet at designated testing locations. DSST testing facilities are located at more than 500 military installations, so service members on active duty can get a jump-start on a post-military career with the DSST program. As an additional incentive, DANTES (Defense Activity for Non-Traditional Education Support) provides funding for DSST test fees for eligible members of the military.

More than 30 subject-matter tests are available in the fields of Business, Humanities, Math, Physical Science, Social Sciences, and Technology.

Available DSST® Exams

Business	Social Sciences
Business Ethics and Society	A History of the Vietnam War
Business Mathematics	Art of the Western World
Computing and Information Technology	Criminal Justice
Human Resource Management	Foundations of Education
Introduction to Business	Fundamentals of Counseling
Management Information Systems	General Anthropology
Money and Banking	History of the Soviet Union
Organizational Behavior	Introduction to Geography
Personal Finance	Introduction to Law Enforcement
Principles of Finance	Lifespan Developmental Psychology
Principles of Supervision	Substance Abuse
	The Civil War and Reconstruction

Humanities	Physical Sciences
Ethics in America	Astronomy
Introduction to World Religions	Environmental Science
Principles of Advanced English	Health and Human Development
Composition	Introduction to Geology
Principles of Public Speaking	

Math	Technology
Fundamentals of College Algebra	Ethics in Technology
Math for Liberal Arts	Fundamentals of Cybersecurity
Principles of Statistics	Technical Writing

As you can see from the table, the DSST program covers a wide variety of subjects. However, it is important to ask two questions before registering for a DSST exam.

1. Which universities or colleges award credit for passing DSST exams?
2. Which DSST exams are the most relevant to my desired degree and my experience?

Knowing which universities offer DSST credit is important. In all likelihood, a college in your area awards credit for DSST exams, but find out before taking an exam by contacting the university directly. Then review the list of DSST exams to determine which ones are most relevant to the degree you are seeking and to your base of knowledge. Schedule an appointment with your college adviser to determine which exams best fit your degree program and which college courses the DSST exams can replace. Advisers should also be able to tell you the minimum score required on the DSST exam to receive university credit.

DSST® TEST CENTERS

You can find DSST testing locations in community colleges and universities across the country. Check the DSST website (**www.getcollegecredit.com**) for a location near you or contact your local college or university to find out if the school administers DSST exams. Keep in mind that some universities and colleges administer DSST exams only to enrolled students. DSST testing is available to men and women in the armed services at more than 500 military installations around the world.

HOW TO REGISTER FOR A DSST® EXAM

Once you have located a nearby DSST testing facility, you need to contact the testing center to find out the exam administration schedule. Many centers are set up to administer tests via the internet, while others use printed materials. Almost all DSST exams are available as online tests, but the method used depends on the testing center. The cost for each DSST exam starts at $100, and many testing locations charge a fee to cover their costs for administering the tests. Credit cards are the only accepted payment method for taking online DSST exams. Credit card, certified check, and money order are acceptable payment methods for paper-and-pencil tests.

Test takers are allotted two score reports—one mailed to them and another mailed to a designated college or university, if requested. Online tests generate unofficial scores at the end of the test session, while individuals taking paper tests must wait four to six weeks for score reports.

PREPARING FOR A DSST® EXAM

Even though you are knowledgeable in a certain subject matter, you should still prepare for the test to ensure you achieve the highest score possible. The first step in studying for a DSST exam is to find out what will be on the specific test you have chosen. Information regarding test content is located on the DSST fact sheets, which can be downloaded at no cost from www.getcollegecredit.com. Each fact sheet outlines the topics covered on a subject-matter test, as well as the approximate percentage assigned to each topic. For example, questions on the Principles of Public Speaking exam are distributed in the following way: Ethical, Social, and Theoretical Considerations of Public Speaking—9%, Audience Analysis, Adaptation, and Effect—15%, Topics and Purposes of Speech—9%, Structure/Organization—17%, Content—17%, Research—11%, Language and Style—9%, and Delivery—13%.

In addition to the breakdown of topics on a DSST exam, the fact sheet also lists recommended reference materials. If you do not own the recommended books, then check college bookstores. Avoid paying high prices for new textbooks by looking online for used textbooks. Don't panic if you are unable to locate a specific textbook listed on the fact sheet; the textbooks are merely recommendations. Instead, search for comparable books used in university courses on the specific subject. Current editions are ideal, and it is a good idea to use at least two references when studying for a DSST exam. Of course, the subject matter provided in this book will be a sufficient review for most test takers. However, if you need additional information, then it is a good idea to have some of the reference materials at your disposal when preparing for a DSST exam.

Fact sheets include other useful information in addition to a list of reference materials and topics. Each fact sheet includes subject-specific sample questions like those you will encounter on the DSST exam. The sample questions provide an idea of the types of questions you can expect on the exam. Test questions are multiple-choice with one correct answer and three incorrect choices.

The fact sheet also includes information about the number of credit hours that ACE has recommended be awarded by colleges for a passing DSST exam score. However, you should keep in mind that not all universities and colleges adhere to the ACE recommendation for DSST credit hours. Some institutions require DSST exam scores higher than the minimum score recommended by ACE. Once you have acquired appropriate reference materials and you have the outline provided on the fact sheet, you are ready to start studying, which is where this book can help.

TEST DAY

After reviewing the material and taking practice tests, you are finally ready to take your DSST exam. Follow these tips for a successful test day experience.

1. **Arrive on time.** Not only is it courteous to arrive on time to the DSST testing facility, but it also allows plenty of time for you to take care of check-in procedures and settle into your surroundings.

2. **Bring identification.** DSST test facilities require that candidates bring a valid government-issued identification card with a current photo and signature. Acceptable forms of identification include a current driver's license, passport, military identification card, or state-issued identification card. Individuals who fail to bring proper identification to the DSST testing facility will not be allowed to take an exam.

3. **Bring the right supplies.** If your exam requires the use of a calculator, you may bring a calculator that meets the specifications. For paper-based exams, you may also bring No. 2 pencils with an eraser and black ballpoint pens. Regardless of the exam methodology, you are NOT allowed to bring reference or study materials, scratch paper, or electronics such as cell phones, personal handheld devices, cameras, alarm wrist watches, or tape recorders to the testing center.

4. **Take the test.** During the exam, take the time to read each question-and-answer option carefully. Eliminate the choices you know are incorrect to narrow the number of potential answers. If a question completely stumps you, take an educated guess and move on—remember that DSSTs are timed; you will have 2 hours to take the exam.

With the proper preparation, DSST exams will save you both time and money. So join the thousands of people who have already reaped the benefits of DSST exams and move closer than ever to your college degree.

PRINCIPLES OF PUBLIC SPEAKING EXAM FACTS

The DSST® Principles of Public Speaking exam is unique. The exam is divided into two parts and contains 100 questions to be answered in 2 hours. Part 1 contains multiple-choice questions covering audience analysis; topics and purposes of speeches; structure and organization; content and supporting materials; research; language and style; delivery; adaptation and effect; and ethical, social, and theoretical considerations. Part 2 requires you to record an impromptu persuasive speech that will be scored by a faculty member who teaches public speaking at an accredited college or university. The person scoring your speech will use a scoring rubric containing these five elements: structure and organization (25%); delivery (25%); content and supporting material (20%); effect and persuasiveness (20%); and language and style (10%). You will have 20 minutes to complete Part 2 with 5 minutes to record your speech.

Area or Course Equivalent: Principles of Public Speaking
Level: Lower-level baccalaureate
Amount of Credit: 3 Semester Hours
Minimum Score: 400
Source: https://www.getcollegecredit.com/wp-content/assets/factsheets/PrinciplesOfPublicSpeaking.pdf

I. **Ethical, Social, and Theoretical Considerations of Public Speaking – 9%**

   a. E.g. Free speech

II. **Audience Analysis, Adaptation, and Effect – 15%**

   a. Analyzing the audience before, during, and after the speech

III. **Topics and Purposes of Speeches – 9%**

   a. Formulating appropriate speech topics for specific purposes

IV. **Structure/Organization – 17%**

   a. E.g. "the hook", structuring introductions, bodies, and conclusions

V. **Content – 17%**

   a. E.g. Recognizing/using argument, reasoning, and evidence

VI. **Research – 11%**

   a. Using reference materials/ finding appropriate sources in speech preparation

VII. **Language and Style – 9%**

   a. Using language appropriate for a public speech

VIII. **Delivery – 13%**

   a. E.g. articulation, voice, pronunciation, body language, and media

Chapter 2

Principles of Public Speaking Diagnostic Test

DIAGNOSTIC TEST ANSWER SHEET

1. Ⓐ Ⓑ Ⓒ Ⓓ

2. Ⓐ Ⓑ Ⓒ Ⓓ

3. Ⓐ Ⓑ Ⓒ Ⓓ

4. Ⓐ Ⓑ Ⓒ Ⓓ

5. Ⓐ Ⓑ Ⓒ Ⓓ

6. Ⓐ Ⓑ Ⓒ Ⓓ

7. Ⓐ Ⓑ Ⓒ Ⓓ

8. Ⓐ Ⓑ Ⓒ Ⓓ

9. Ⓐ Ⓑ Ⓒ Ⓓ

10. Ⓐ Ⓑ Ⓒ Ⓓ

11. Ⓐ Ⓑ Ⓒ Ⓓ

12. Ⓐ Ⓑ Ⓒ Ⓓ

13. Ⓐ Ⓑ Ⓒ Ⓓ

14. Ⓐ Ⓑ Ⓒ Ⓓ

15. Ⓐ Ⓑ Ⓒ Ⓓ

16. Ⓐ Ⓑ Ⓒ Ⓓ

17. Ⓐ Ⓑ Ⓒ Ⓓ

18. Ⓐ Ⓑ Ⓒ Ⓓ

19. Ⓐ Ⓑ Ⓒ Ⓓ

20. Ⓐ Ⓑ Ⓒ Ⓓ

PRINCIPLES OF PUBLIC SPEAKING DIAGNOSTIC TEST

24 minutes—20 questions

Directions: Carefully read each of the following 20 questions. Choose the best answer to each question and fill in the corresponding circle on the answer sheet. The Answer Key and Explanations can be found following this Diagnostic Test.

---

1. When writing your speech, which of the following would be a good way to narrow or focus a topic choice?

   A. Topoi
   B. Brainstorming
   C. A tree diagram
   D. Surveys

2. In the US, the First Amendment ensures that speech is

   A. always protected, regardless of content.
   B. not protected all of the time.
   C. protected if it's not broadcast.
   D. never protected.

3. Which of the following might be used as a narrative for supporting material?

   A. An example of how MP3 music files sound compared to MP4 files
   B. A story about how the Dodge brothers founded their automobile company
   C. The opinion of a musician about a new recording technique
   D. A startling quotation meant to break the ice when beginning a speech

4. Which of the following is NOT a tool used in audience analysis?

   A. Demographic analysis
   B. Linguistics
   C. Questionnaires
   D. Situational analysis

5. In an interview, asking a closed question is a good way to

    A. get the interviewee to open up about their feelings and values.

    B. find out how the interviewee felt about their childhood.

    C. elicit brief, one- or two-word answers to questions about basic facts.

    D. communicate to the interviewee the fact that you're running short of time.

6. A gazetteer is a

    A. dictionary of foreign terms.

    B. broadsheet containing population data.

    C. geographical dictionary.

    D. dictionary of research terms.

7. The main points of a speech should be constructed as

    A. compound sentences.

    B. infinitive statements.

    C. parallel statements.

    D. rhetorical questions.

8. When using expert testimony from a person who may not be familiar to the audience, it's important to

    A. make the competence of the individual clear to the audience.

    B. place the source's name on the whiteboard, presentation slide, or other display.

    C. discard that testimony since the audience has no idea who the person is.

    D. challenge the testimony to show that you're unbiased.

9. In which of the following is the danger of stereotyping most likely?

    A. Questionnaires

    B. Direct observation

    C. Situational analysis

    D. Psychological analysis

10. Global plagiarism is the act of

    A. stealing from the speech of someone who lives far away.
    B. stealing an entire speech and presenting it as your own.
    C. using someone else's ideas in your speech.
    D. using parts of multiple speeches and combining them into one speech for which you take credit.

11. A good persuasive speech requires

    A. facts, evidence, and other supporting materials.
    B. that the writer agrees with the position he or she takes in a speech.
    C. a strongly held opinion.
    D. familiarity with the topic.

12. The purpose of audience analysis is to

    A. help you memorize your speech.
    B. allow you to adapt your speech to your listener.
    C. improve the logic of your argument.
    D. determine the listeners' attitudes.

13. Which of the following is NOT necessary to do when preparing for an interview?

    A. Determine the purpose of the interview.
    B. Write out intelligent and meaningful questions ahead of time.
    C. Select the specific goal of the speech.
    D. Choose an individual to interview and arrange an appointment.

14. The most effective speeches are written with what in mind?

    A. A specific audience
    B. A general audience
    C. The presenter's field of expertise
    D. The goal of the speech

15. Which type of argument is being used in the following statement? *"Fever and a rash indicate an allergic reaction."*

    A. Argument from causation
    B. Argument from example
    C. Argument from analogy
    D. Argument from sign

16. What is one advantage of a manuscript speech?

    A. Eye contact is maintained.
    B. It's easy to respond to audience feedback.
    C. It may sound awkward or stilted.
    D. Timing can be controlled.

17. The introduction should

    A. make up about 20 percent of the entire speech.
    B. include a rhetorical question.
    C. gain the attention of the audience.
    D. clarify what listeners should do in response to the speech.

18. An informative speech attempts to

    A. persuade a listener.
    B. amuse a listener.
    C. explain something to a listener.
    D. convince a listener of something.

19. Because people listening to a speech often struggle to follow along with a written copy, it's best to

    A. keep the language simple and use only short words.
    B. use connectives and many concrete and familiar words.
    C. use as many abstract words as possible.
    D. keep the speech brief so as not to confuse listeners.

20. Adding sounds to words where they do not belong is a problem associated with

    A. articulation.
    B. pronunciation.
    C. pauses.
    D. proxemics.

ANSWER KEY AND EXPLANATIONS

1. C	5. C	9. B	13. C	17. C
2. B	6. C	10. B	14. A	18. C
3. B	7. C	11. A	15. D	19. B
4. B	8. A	12. B	16. D	20. A

1. **The correct answer is C.** All four options are good tools for topic selection, but only a tree diagram is specifically meant to help you narrow your choice of topic.

2. **The correct answer is B.** Not all speech is protected all the time. Speech that is untrue, inflammatory, or seen as a danger to the community may be proscribed. Whether the speech is broadcast, printed, or spoken is irrelevant.

3. **The correct answer is B.** A narrative is a *story*. Examples (choice A) and opinions (choice C) often make good supporting material, but choice B is the best choice for supporting material in this case. A startling quotation (choice D) sometimes makes a good opening for a speech, but it's not normally supporting material, nor is it a story.

4. **The correct answer is B.** Linguistics is the study of language. Knowledge of language might play a part in crafting your speech, but it is not an audience analysis tool, as are the other three options.

5. **The correct answer is C.** The point of a closed question (e.g., *In what year were you born? In what state?*) is to elicit brief answers to basic questions. You would use open questions (e.g., *How do you feel about what's happened in the state politically?*) to get the interviewee to open up about their feelings or values (choice A) or childhood (choice B). You would never ask questions designed to hurry the interviewee along because you're running out of time (choice D).

6. **The correct answer is C.** A gazetteer is a geographic dictionary. It is generally used with a map or atlas and presents information about the social and geographical makeup of a region or country.

7. **The correct answer is C.** Main points of a speech should be written in a parallel grammatical structure; each statement should be phrased in a similar way. Although writing a main point as a compound sentence (choice A) is acceptable, it's not required, and it does not necessarily imply parallelism. Infinitive statements (choice B) are appropriate for specific purpose statements. Rhetorical questions (choice D) are often used in introductions to encourage listeners to consider a concept or an idea.

8. **The correct answer is A.** Since your audience has not heard of this person, it's important to make sure they realize that the expert knows their subject. You might do this by citing the person's experience or educational background. You may choose to display the expert's name (choice B), but that's not as important as showing that they are competent to comment on this subject. You certainly wouldn't want to discard the expert's opinion (choice C) or challenge it (choice D).

9. **The correct answer is B.** It's possible to stereotype based on any of these, if you're willing to make the leap in logic. But the one that's *most* likely to lead to stereotyping is direct observation: it would be easy to make judgments based on what you see when you *look at* (observe) your audience, and those judgments may be flawed, based on what you assume about what you see.

10. **The correct answer is B.** Global plagiarism is the act of stealing the entirety of another's work. Where your source lives (choice A) is irrelevant, and stealing the source's words or ideas is plagiarism in one form or another. Using someone else's ideas (choice C) is known as incremental plagiarism. Using multiple parts of multiple speeches verbatim (choice D) is known as patchwork plagiarism.

11. **The correct answer is A.** A persuasive speech cannot be effective unless its claims are supported by evidence—facts, examples, statistics, etc. Choice B is incorrect because it's not necessary to agree with a position to argue it; in fact, arguing against (or for) a position in which you do (or do not) believe is excellent training in rhetoric, speechmaking, or debate. Similarly, choices C and D are incorrect because you need not hold a strong opinion or

be familiar with the topic in order to argue for or against something—although in the case of choice D, you will probably have to gain some familiarity with the topic through your research.

12. **The correct answer is B.** The purpose of audience analysis is to help you adapt your speech, modifying it so that it's effective with a specific audience. Analyzing your audience would have little bearing on helping you memorize your speech, nor would it necessarily affect the logic of your argument, thereby eliminating choices A and C. While you may wish to determine the attitudes of your listeners as a part of your analysis, choice D is incorrect because the purpose of that determination of attitude would be to help you adapt the speech.

13. **The correct answer is C.** While you may have selected the specific goal of the speech, it's not absolutely necessary to have done so; in fact, you may be interviewing as part of a process to help you select that goal. However, you do need to decide on the purpose of the interview (choice A), write out your questions (choice B), and arrange/schedule the interview ahead of time (choice D).

14. **The correct answer is A.** The best speeches are ones that are tailored to a particular audience. The goal is definitely important, but a clear goal may still result in an ineffective speech if the speech is not audience centered.

15. **The correct answer is D.** An argument from sign cites information that signals a claim. A fever and a rash typically accompany allergic reactions, so they are signs of an allergic reaction. The rash and fever did not cause the allergic reaction, so choice A is incorrect. An argument from example (choice B), supports a claim with examples, while an argument from analogy (choice C) supports a claim with a comparable situation.

16. **The correct answer is D.** With a manuscript speech, it's easy to control the timing, because you can deliver the exact same speech during practice until you get the timing where you want it; if you need a speech of exactly four minutes, you can write and practice it so that it takes exactly that long to deliver. While eye contact is very desirable, choice A is incorrect because the inability to

maintain eye contact is considered a disadvantage of reading from a manuscript. Similarly, the opposite of choice B is true. It's very difficult to respond to feedback when reading a speech. The fact that the speech may sound awkward is considered a disadvantage, not an advantage of reading a speech from a prepared manuscript.

17. **The correct answer is C.** The introduction needs to grab the attention of your listeners. It generally makes up about 10 percent of the speech, not 20 percent as choice A erroneously indicates. Though it is a good approach to throw in a rhetorical question, choice B is not the best answer because it is not necessary to include one in the introduction. Choice D doesn't make sense. The introduction of a speech usually does not clarify what the listeners should do in response to the speech, because they've not yet heard the speech.

18. **The correct answer is C.** An informative speech explains. While the new information presented could persuade listeners to act or think in a certain way and the speech may be somewhat amusing, the primary purpose of an informative speech is to inform.

19. **The correct answer is B.** Effective speeches tend to use concrete words that refer to tangible objects because they're easy to visualize. It's also good to use connectives as a way of making sure the audience is following along as you move from one idea, point, or topic to another. It's not necessary to use simple language (choice A), unless your audience requires it (for example, you're speaking to elementary school students). Using abstract words (choice C) tends to make a speech *more* difficult to understand, which is why concrete terms are recommended. You may wish to keep your speech brief (choice D), but that's a function of the topic and your audience analysis, not because the audience may struggle to follow along with a written copy.

20. **The correct answer is A.** Adding sounds where they do not belong is an articulation problem; a speaker might say ath-a-lete instead of ath-lete, for example. Choice B is related to errors in accentuation and the pronunciation of silent sounds. Filled and unfilled pauses (choice C) are typical of many speeches, but do not involve adding sounds to words. Proxemics (choice D) refers to how space is used by a speaker during a presentation.

DIAGNOSTIC TEST ASSESSMENT GRID

Now that you've completed the diagnostic test and read through the answer explanations, you can use your results to target your studying. Find the question numbers from the diagnostic test that you answered incorrectly and highlight or circle them below. Then focus extra attention on the sections dealing with those topics.

Principles of Public Speaking	
Content Area	Question #
Ethical, Social, and Theoretical Considerations	2, 10
Audience Analysis, Adaptation, and Effect	4, 9, 12, 14
Topics and Purposes of Speeches	1, 18
Structure/Organization	7, 15, 17
Content/Supporting Materials	3, 5, 8, 13
Research	6, 11
Language and Style	19
Delivery	16, 20

Chapter 3

Principles of Public Speaking Subject Review

OVERVIEW
- Ethical, Social, and Theoretical Considerations of Public Speaking
- Audience Analysis and Adaptation
- Speech Topics and Purposes
- Research and Content
- Organizing Your Speech
- Language and Style
- Delivering Your Speech
- Summing It Up

ETHICAL, SOCIAL, AND THEORETICAL CONSIDERATIONS OF PUBLIC SPEAKING

Public speaking is simply one aspect of what's known more generally as **communication skills**. Knowing how to deliver a speech is not just a theoretical or intellectual exercise; it's very practical, and knowing how to speak in public will serve you well not only in your academic career, but also at work, at home, and with friends and colleagues.

Many people fear public speaking, but you don't have to. If you have a well-crafted speech and you've practiced delivering that speech, you have little to worry about. It's all about confidence, and if your speech is solid and you know some of the "tricks of the trade," you will have the confidence you need to deliver it effectively. This chapter will help you develop both your skills and your confidence.

The good news is that if you've ever taken a writing or rhetoric course, you already know much of what you'll need to craft a good speech. Many of the same skills and methods used to create a good story or fashion a cohesive argument on paper are exactly the same ones you will use to create an entertaining or persuasive speech; the main difference is that a speech is the final product rather than a paper or essay. So if many of the topics discussed here look familiar to you, consider this a chance to brush-up your current skills and an opportunity to learn how to use those skills in a new way.

Ethics in Public Speaking

We may not always stop to realize it, but there is an ethical component to speaking in public. In other words, when delivering a speech (as when writing a paper), there are issues of morality and fairness to consider, and those issues are present at every stage of the process—from selecting your topic to researching your speech and from analyzing your audience to delivering the speech.

In the United States, the First Amendment protects freedom of speech, but both law and common sense have long determined that not *all* speech is protected all the time; after all, some of that speech might be unfair, some might be untrue, some might be harmful, and the goals of some forms of speech may run counter to the goals of the society in which you live.

When the Greek philosopher Aristotle considered the speaker's role in public speaking, he referred to the concept of **ethos**, by which he meant the "character and credibility" of the speaker. In terms of public speaking, what he meant was that there are certain moral considerations to a speech or any communication for that matter.

- Are the goals of the speech ethically sound?
- Is the subject matter appropriate for the audience?
- Is the information accurate and appropriately cited?

If you can answer all of these questions in the affirmative, then both your speech and the person delivering the speech are considered credible. Aristotle would have said that the requirements of ethos have been met. If you are instead delivering a speech that evokes strong feelings for an immoral purpose (consider Hitler's use of hatred toward Jews to encourage German support of his actions or the use of name-calling to degrade people based on their ethnicity, sexual orientation, or religion) then your ethos is suspect. Aristotle would have said that your ethos—and therefore your credibility—are lacking.

Plagiarism

Perhaps the most obvious form of unethical speechwriting is **plagiarism**, which is the theft of another person's words or ideas. This can occur in any of three ways:

1. **Global plagiarism** occurs when an entire speech is stolen from a source, and the speaker presents the work as his or her own.
2. **Patchwork plagiarism** involves stealing from a number of sources, rather than from a single source. A speaker might copy word for word from multiple sources and then combine them into a single speech, for which he or she takes full credit.
3. **Incremental plagiarism** is subtler and sometimes difficult to recognize. Instead of stealing sections of another's work verbatim, the speechwriter incorporates direct quotations in a speech or paraphrases the unique ideas of another person without giving proper credit. Both are considered plagiarism unless the original source is cited during the speech.

How can you know when an idea is uniquely yours or whether it came from elsewhere? It's not always easy to tell when you might be plagiarizing, but when in doubt, *cite*. The citation doesn't have to be complicated or clumsy; simply insert a quick reference into your speech. For example, you could insert something like, "*As Dr. Olen Davis noted in a recent Stanford University study*, chimpanzees raised in a non-nurturing environment seem to become non-nurturers themselves, showing little affection for their offspring." In this example, the italicized portion is your citation.

The bottom line is that any form of plagiarism is ethically unacceptable. It's a form of thievery; by taking credit for others' words or ideas, you're denying them credit (and sometimes payment) for what is rightfully theirs.

AUDIENCE ANALYSIS AND ADAPTATION

Imagine a conversation between two experienced photographers:

> **Photographer 1:** Well, it's a good setup, but I'm not sure the depth of field is going to work. I'd really like to see some circles of confusion behind those highlights. Otherwise, we'll be going all F/64 school—I don't think that'd work here.

> **Photographer 2:** Wouldn't you think that sort of bokeh would detract? Maybe distract the viewer?

Photographer 1: No, I wouldn't worry about that. As long as we're following the rule of thirds, the viewer will look where we want him to. I'm a bit more worried about the lighting—you know, the inverse square law. I'd want to be careful about keeping the background correctly exposed without blowing out the highlights in her face. Maybe a balloon reflector off to one side? That kind of catchlight might also add some nice highlights in the eyes, too.

Photographer 2: I think that'd help a lot! And if we start at F/2.8 and then bracket as we close down, we can shoot reciprocals; that should get us some we can use.

It's obvious that these two photographers understand one another and the photography techniques they are discussing. They are each an appropriate audience for what the other is saying. However, that conversation would make little sense to anyone who is not familiar with photography or photographic techniques.

Audience knowledge of a subject plays a major role in the language and terminology used in a speech. *Your* audience may not be familiar with your subject, so you need to learn about your audience and then tailor your speech to fit that audience.

In fact, your speech should be largely **audience-centered**; in other words, crafted specifically for your audience. The audience is your *primary* consideration when writing and delivering a speech. You don't want to be speaking over their heads; the audience might not understand you. But you also don't want to "dumb it down" too much; that would be insulting, not to mention boring. You need to understand your audience, identify with them, and get them on your side. This is known as **audience identification**, the process of forming a bond with listeners. You can do that by acquiring information about the audience's background and attitudes, and that knowledge will help you adapt your speech.

Speakers can learn about listeners in a number of ways:
- Direct observation
- Questionnaires
- Demographic analysis
- Situational analysis
- Psychological analysis

Direct Observation

Direct observation of your audience is the simplest, most straightforward way to gather information about your listeners. You can learn a lot about your audience by observing. What do you see? What do you hear? What do you smell? By observing with the five natural senses, you can gather some basic information about their appearance, age, or ethnicity. But watch out because there's a danger here. It's very easy to stereotype or make assumptions.

Questionnaires

Depending on the situation, you may be able to gather information about your audience through a **questionnaire**. Questionnaires distributed via email prior to a speech can help a speaker determine the attitudes and knowledge base of audience members regarding a particular topic. This method is often used for classroom speeches.

Demographic Analysis

A **demographic analysis** lets you learn about listeners based on demographic factors, including age, gender, religion, sexual orientation, ethnicity, economic status, occupation, education, and organizational membership. Like direct observation, it can be easy to fall into stereotypes when using demographic analysis, so watch out for that. On the other hand, this sort of analysis *does* allow us to make certain types of assumptions. For example, the age of audience members can have a significant impact on many aspects of a speech. An older audience would most likely be more interested in a speech about estate planning than about dating issues. In addition to guiding the speech topic, age also affects the information presented in the speech. An older audience would be more likely understand historical references to World War II or the Great Depression, while a younger audience may require additional background information.

Situational Analysis

A **situational analysis** considers the characteristics of a particular audience, such as size, physical setting, occasion, and time. The size of an audience affects speech delivery; a small audience can be addressed informally, while a large audience requires more structure. Moreover, a large audience prevents a speaker from assessing how listeners are responding to a speech because of the distance between the speaker and each audience member. Flexibility during speech presentation is essential to adapting to audience size, which may be unknown until moments before the speech begins. The setting of a speech may be a classroom, a crowded auditorium, or a large dining hall, and unpleasant settings require speakers to remain energetic in order to hold the interest of listeners.

The audience and occasion of a speech are important situational factors to consider. The tone and content of a pep-rally speech to a company's sales team is different from that of a presentation to stockholders. Time is another situational factor and refers to both the time of day and the length of the speech. Speakers often find listeners attentive in the morning and tired late in the afternoon, which is a consideration when determining the length of a speech. Experts speaking at conventions, for example, always dread being assigned the 4:00 p.m. slot; the audience is tired and thinking about dinner. Speakers with the most clout (i.e., the best reputations and who are the most powerful draw) are usually assigned something close to the 10:00 a.m. slot. At that time, listeners tend to be focused and alert. They've had breakfast, it's not quite lunchtime, the day is young, and their brain isn't too tired or overstimulated. Think about your own experience taking that late afternoon/early evening class; it was often difficult to concentrate, wasn't it?

Psychological Analysis

A **psychological analysis** seeks to determine whether audiences are willing to listen to the speaker, whether they view your topic or thesis in a favorable or unfavorable light, and whether they're knowledgeable about the topic. The answer to each of these will affect how you write and deliver your speech. If the audience is interested and they are attending voluntarily (they may even have *paid* to attend), you should have little trouble. But if they were *forced* to attend (perhaps for a class or work requirement), then you have to work to *make* them more willing. Use humor or startling examples to get their attention. Reward them for their attendance—let them know that you are aware of and appreciate their sacrifice. Do this *first*, before getting to the main topic of your speech. Show your audience how your topic relates to them and to their needs. In all of these cases, what you've done is connected with your audience and given them a good reason to listen.

Adaptation

All of this analysis is simply to allow you to *adapt* your message to make it appropriate for a specific audience. **Audience adaptation** occurs when preparing the speech *and* when presenting the speech. During the speech-writing process, the information gained from the audience analysis directs topic selection, determines examples to use, and guides the phrasing of introductions and conclusions. Audience adaptation is an important part of creating an audience-centered speech—one that is crafted for your specific audience and which takes their knowledge and attitudes into account. Every stage of the speechmaking process should consider audience response to the message. During the writing phase, a speaker modifies a speech to make it as coherent and appropriate as possible for the expected audience. During speech presentations, effective speakers make adaptations based on feedback from the given audience. For example, a speaker who presents a concept and notices confused looks on the faces of many listeners may review the idea again or rephrase the information in a different way. (This is one reason to make frequent eye contact during a speech; it helps you gather real-time feedback about how your message is being received. We'll address eye contact in more depth later.) Successful public speakers use audience analysis to adapt to audiences both before and during speeches.

SPEECH TOPICS AND PURPOSES

As with writing a paper, there are three possible purposes of a speech:

1. To inform
2. To persuade
3. To entertain

An **informative speech** seeks to increase audience awareness and understanding of a subject. This kind of speech does not try to persuade listeners to respond or act, but a **persuasive speech** does exactly that: you're trying to change your listeners' attitudes, beliefs, or behaviors. The main purpose of an **entertaining speech** is, not surprisingly, simply to use humor and cleverness to amuse.

Note that these purposes can sometimes overlap. It is very possible to use humor and wit as a way of changing someone's beliefs or persuading them to take some action. It's equally possible to inform listeners in an entertaining fashion, while at the same time hoping to persuade them. Still, it helps to think of the purpose of your speech as predominantly informative, persuasive, or entertaining—while keeping in mind the possibility of some overlap.

Of course, every speech needs a topic, and there are many ways to generate topic ideas. Sometimes, as when an instructor or supervisor assigns you a topic (*Joanne, would you address the Board of Directors at the next meeting and explain to them how our supply chain works?*), you simply have no real choice of topic.

Sources of Topics

Usually, though, you'll need to come up with a topic and there are plenty of possible sources. You might start by looking at **surveys**, such as the Gallup Poll, which can provide you with topic ideas related to current issues, trends, or problems. Newspapers and magazines, such as *Time*, *Newsweek*, and *Forbes*, can provide information about current events and issues people are concerned about.

Brainstorming is another topic-selection tool, one that works especially well when there are two or more people involved. You simply throw out ideas, preferably as quickly as possible, while someone jots them down in a notepad or on a marker board. The only rule is that there's no such thing as a bad idea—*everything* gets written down, even if it sounds silly; sometimes these "silly" ideas lead to good ones, and sometimes the silly one turns out not to be silly at all.

A **tree diagram** can also help you generate a topic; it's an especially good way to help you focus on or narrow a topic. You simply write a topic idea on a "branch," and then repeatedly divide that first topic into smaller and smaller parts until you arrive at a manageable topic. You can do the same thing by placing topics into "bubbles" and then drawing more bubbles off of that main one, and then more off of those smaller bubbles, etc. This approach is sometimes called **mind mapping**. If you were going to speak about motorcycles, for example, you might realize right away that "motorcycles" is much too broad a topic for a brief speech; you could write an entire book—or several books—about motorcycles. But you might be able to narrow that topic by using a tree diagram or mind map. If you did, you might end up with a much more manageable motorcycle-related topic such as "helmets" in this fashion:

Motorcycles → Safety → Safety Gear → Helmets

If you know (or would like to learn) about motorcycle helmets, you can certainly deliver a focused 5- or 10-minute speech on that topic much more easily than trying to cram everything there is to know about motorcycles into one speech.

A fourth way to generate topic ideas is to use **topoi**. This method is based on ancient rhetorical techniques (back to Aristotle again) and involves asking and answering questions in order to generate topic ideas by stimulating creative thinking. The word *topoi* comes from *topos* and means a collection of stock topics used in rhetoric as subjects for argument. It has since come to mean generating topics in a broader sense. Ask yourself some questions about your general subject area: *Who? What? Why? When? Where? How? So?* For example, if we start with drug addiction as our main subject, we might ask these questions: Who is the addict? What does addiction really mean? Why did that person become an addict? When did it happen? Where did it happen? How did they become addicted? What does it mean; that is, *so?* (i.e., Who cares? Should I care?)

You can see how this sort of dialog can lead to some very penetrating questions, which can in turn lead to excellent topic ideas.

After you develop a list of topics all possible speech subjects should be evaluated to determine which one is most appropriate. Topics should be

- interesting to the speaker; otherwise, your lack of enthusiasm will be apparent to listeners.
- interesting and useful to the audience, which can be determined through an audience analysis.
- ethically appropriate.
- appropriate for the specific occasion, which means that the speech should meet audience expectations, be relevant, and be narrow in scope.

In general, topics that are interesting and appropriate for the speaker, the audience, and the occasion make the most effective speeches.

General Purpose, Specific Purpose, and Goals

Once you've established a topic and a general purpose, it's time to think about the specific purpose of your speech—i.e., your exact goal. What are you trying to *do* with this speech, exactly? It helps to have a **specific purpose statement** that focuses on one clear idea and can be stated in a brief infinitive phrase—that is, stated with the word *to* followed by a verb. For example, "to explain how a recycling plant works," "to inform listeners about their choices in the upcoming election," or "to persuade my audience to stop texting while driving." Specific purpose statements guide the direction of the speech, and they serve as one of the most critical early steps of the speechmaking process.

The specific purpose statement leads into the **thesis statement**, which is the central idea or theme of the speech. Does this sound familiar? It should. It's exactly the same way you might write an essay or paper, by using a thesis statement to explain to your reader—in this case, the listener—what you want your audience to learn.

Just as in writing an essay, the thesis statement of an informative speech should be neutral, while the thesis statement of a persuasive speech should express a clear opinion. The following are examples of thesis statements:

- Informative: *There are three primary causes of heart disease.*
- Persuasive: *All high school athletes should be drug-tested.*

The formation of the specific statement of purpose occurs early in the speechwriting process, but the thesis statement typically develops only after you have researched and analyzed the topic. A well-written thesis statement helps develop main ideas for a speech, and it focuses audience attention.

For informative speeches, the thesis is most often stated early in the presentation. For persuasive speeches, the time to introduce your thesis statement depends on the audience. If an audience analysis has determined that listeners are neutral or positive toward the speech topic, then clearly stating the thesis early in the presentation is appropriate. If the audience of a persuasive speech is most likely hostile to the speaker's position, then arguments and evidence should be provided *before* gradually presenting the thesis.

RESEARCH AND CONTENT

In some ways, this is the most difficult part of writing a speech (or a paper). We're used to "arguing" off the top of our heads; we know what we think, and we want the listener to think that way too. If we don't have enough information to convince them, we simply get *louder*. Pretty soon, what started out as a rational discussion or argument turns ugly. It's no longer an argument, it's a fight.

Speech topics require research and planning; that's why this is the difficult part of the process. We may not be used to doing research, to having to come up with facts and examples, to finding factual evidence to convince our listeners. You generally can't simply use the force of your strongly held opinion to make someone believe as you do. If the speech topic is an area familiar to the writer, then life stories and personal experiences make excellent additions to any presentation. However, most speeches cannot rely solely on the expertise of the speaker, so supplemental information needs to be gathered.

One more thing to note about research: If you're doing it right, you will always end up with *too much* information. There will be data, quotes, facts, and general information that you simply don't need. Of course, you won't know that until you begin writing your speech. But you will find that if you've done the "legwork" (i.e., the research), writing the speech will be fairly straightforward. If you run into trouble while writing, it will almost always be because you didn't do enough research. So too much information is exactly what you want; you don't have to use it, of course, but if it's not there, you'll miss it.

TIP: Research and gather as much evidence as you can. The more evidence you have to support your speech topic, the more credible you will be.

Library vs. the Internet

It's the age of the internet. To find information, we rely on digital devices and on data stored on servers thousands of miles away. And we have millions of websites, blogs, and online news media that we can use when we seek information.

And yet, for a number of reasons, the library remains the primary place to go when we need information, partly because the library houses both types of information sources—print and electronic. Also, the print information in a library (especially in the research sections) tends to be *vetted*; it's usually evaluated and scrutinized prior to making it into print. There's nothing magic about this. It's just that printing costs a lot of money, and people—namely publishers and printers—usually want to make sure that what they're about to publish meets certain standards. Thus, print content in a library tends to have been checked over pretty thoroughly. This is not always the case with online sources. But more about that shortly.

Even in the digital age, you can find a number of excellent sources at your local (or school) library:

- Books
- Periodical databases
- Newspapers
- Encyclopedias
- Government publications
- Quotation books
- Biographical aids
- Atlases and gazetteers

If the topic of a speech has been a significant issue for at least six months, then it is highly likely that information can be located in a book. Information regarding more recent issues and topics will be found in periodicals, such as magazines and professional journals, which are published on a regular basis. Periodical databases can help you locate articles from magazines and journals, and these databases typically provide abstracts or summaries of each article. General databases, such as *Reader's Guide to Periodical Literature* and LexisNexis, include popular magazines as well as major academic journals. For topics not covered in general periodicals, search special databases, such as ERIC (the Educational Research Information Center). Libraries keep copies of current issues of local newspapers, and they keep back issues on microfilm or in digital form. LexisNexis and ProQuest are useful tools for locating articles from national and international newspapers. When information is needed about contemporary individuals, biographical aids, such as *Who's Who in America*, can be useful. Atlases, which are books of maps, and gazetteers, which are geographical dictionaries, are resources for facts about places around the world. Another excellent resource for facts about places around the world is the *World Factbook*, published by the Central Intelligence Agency (CIA). The *World Factbook* used to be published only as an actual printed book, but it is now available online (see **https://www.cia.gov/the-world-factbook/**).

Which brings us to the internet. In addition to the library, the internet plays a significant role in modern research, but the accuracy of information is sometimes a concern. The wealth of information available on the internet is extensive, but unlike libraries, the internet lacks quality control mechanisms. The reality is that, while it takes money and skill and a certain level of investment to print a book or newspaper, just about anyone can publish anything they want on the world wide web, basically at no cost. There are no barriers to entry there, as there are in traditional publishing. In many ways this is good. The internet has democratized information; unfortunately, it's also democratized *misinformation*.

There are search engines of course, including Google, DuckDuckGo, and Yahoo, and they can help you find almost anything. But these search engines merely *index* web pages, they do not *evaluate* those pages. Instead, that evaluation is up to you. Wikipedia is an interesting experiment in the democratization of information. Anyone can write a Wikipedia article, and anyone can edit those articles. The site can definitely contain biased or erroneous information; however, errors tend over time to get weeded out by others who come along and improve or remove the questionable data. As a result, Wikipedia is not a bad place to start your research; just don't rely on it exclusively. Be sure to check out the references listed at the bottom of any articles; those usually point to excellent source materials.

Conducting Interviews

Research interviews are another useful tool for gathering information for speeches. Depending on the topic, college professors, business professionals, physicians, psychologists, and engineers can all offer expertise, information, and opinions that may prove useful and interesting.

In order for an interview to be successful, you'll need to do the following:
- Determine the purpose of the interview.
- Write out questions that are intelligent and meaningful.
- Choose an individual to interview and arrange an appointment.

During an interview, it is important to remain flexible and attentive. Follow-up questions help gain additional information from primary questions, which are prepared in advance. **Open questions** (*Why did you become a police officer?*) are broad questions designed to discover the interviewee's values and perspectives, and they tend to elicit long, rambling answers. These are questions to which it is impossible to give one- or two-word answers. Let the interviewee talk; sometimes they will go off on a tangent that turns out to be interesting and useful. Obviously, you don't have to use everything the interviewee says, so you're free to pick and choose. But keep in mind that you can't selectively use quotes taken out of context to advance your own agenda or bolster your own opinion; doing so would be unethical. In contrast, **closed questions** (*Where were you born?*) elicit brief answers. Being appropriately dressed, arriving on time, and maintaining the purpose of the interview all show respect for the interviewee's time. Taking accurate notes or recording the interview ensures that the information gathered will not be lost and that your recollection of the conversation will be accurate. Just be sure to let the interviewee know if you are using a recording device ahead of time, and make sure you have their permission.

TIP: Use open and closed questions to your advantage. If you need more infor-mation or your interviewee is too brief, ask a few open-ended questions. If your interview has strayed off-topic, ask a few closed questions.

Here's an important interviewing trick. When your interview is finished, after you've thanked the interviewee for their time, ask one last follow-up question: *Is there anyone else knowledgeable about this topic that you would recommend I call or email?* You will almost always end your interview with another source of information, and when you call or email that person, you can explain, "so-and-so suggested I speak with you." Having one expert recommend another expert is a gift of sorts; you didn't have to go search out another source, your new source has already been vetted by the expert who recommended them, your new source may be more likely to talk with you, and you have a new resource for future use.

Content and Supporting Materials

As we've discussed, effective speeches require evidence to validate and explain opinions and issues. The evidence comes in the form of **supporting materials**—content that is incorporated into a speech that provides information, maintains listener interest, and asserts persuasive evidence. Supporting materials include examples, narratives, testimonies, statistics, and quotations. Most of these types of supporting materials are fairly obvious, but let's break them down, just for the sake of clarity.

- **Narratives** are stories told to illustrate a concept or point. Narratives help illus-trate abstract ideas, and they come in three basic types: explanatory, exemplary, and persuasive. As suggested by the names, explanatory narratives explain events, exemplary narratives are examples of excellence (such as rags-to-riches stories about famous people), and persuasive narratives attempt to change beliefs or attitudes. An **anecdote** is a brief story that is usually humorous.
- **Examples** are brief, specific instances used to illustrate a point. If the example is long enough and you tell a story about it, it becomes a narrative. Be sure to distinguish between real and hypothetical (imaginary) examples, so as not to confuse or mislead your audience.

- **Testimonies** are the opinions of experts (or, in some cases, eyewitnesses) that support a speaker's claim. Testimonies add substance to a speech. Although personal testimonies can be incorporated into a speech, listeners are generally more persuaded by expert testimonies. When using expert testimonies, it is important to make the competence of the individual clear to the audience, especially if the person's name is unknown to most listeners. The testimony's unbiased nature should be emphasized so that the information will have a significant impact on the audience. Testimonies should also be recent in order to be most effective.

- **Statistics** are verifiable numerical data used to clarify or make a point. The fact that the data is verifiable is important; otherwise, people could just make up numbers to "prove" whatever they wanted you to believe. You can use statistics to illustrate points in informative speeches; in persuasive speeches, statistics serve to provide the basis of claims and arguments. Be sure to use only recent statistics, and only from reliable (and perhaps multiple) sources. Finally, don't overuse them. Nothing will make your listeners' eyes glaze over more quickly than an overwhelming amount of data; the use of only a few interesting numbers is far more effective.

- **Quotations** are verbatim explanations or opinions used in a speech. Naturally, you would cite the source of the quotation: *As British statesman Winston Churchill once said, "In politics when you are in doubt what to do, do nothing ... when you are in doubt what to say, say what you really think."* As with statistics (or really, any supporting material), it's best not to overuse quotations or to use quotations that are too lengthy.

TIP: Be prepared to "share your work"—that is, be able to provide your audience with a list of sources showing where you found your information.

Evaluating Supporting Material

Remember, if you're doing a good job researching, you're going to end up with more information than you can use in this one speech. And that's okay; better too much information than not enough.

So how will you evaluate this material? You can start by subjecting the information to a four-pronged test, asking the following questions:

- Is the information relevant and significant?
- Is it easily understood?
- Is it striking and/or unique?
- Is it credible, ethical, and accurate?

If you're using the internet for research, you might consider using what some teachers call the **CRAAP test**. When you look at a website, ask the following questions:

- **Currency:** Is the material current? When was it published or posted? Has it been recently updated? Do the links work, or have they gone dead?
- **Relevance:** Does the information relate to the topic? Who is the intended audience? Is that audience similar to yours in terms of the level or scope of the information? Could you comfortably cite this material in a research paper?
- **Authority:** What is the source of this information? Can you determine who is the author? The publisher? What are the author's credentials? Is there contact information on the site? Could you contact the writer or publisher if you wanted to? Does the URL reveal anything about the author or publication? (For instance, a *.com* or *.biz* address is commercial, *.org* is usually a nonprofit organization, *.edu* is an educational institution, *.gov* is a government-sponsored website.)
- **Accuracy:** Can you tell if the information is reliable, correct, and truthful? Is there evidence to support the author's contentions? Could you verify that information using another source—or even from personal knowledge?
- **Purpose:** Why is this information there in the first place? Is the site trying to inform? To sell? To entertain? To persuade? Is the information objective and impartial, or can you spot ideological, religious, personal, or other biases?

It's important to keep a healthy skepticism when it comes to information you have pulled from the internet. While the internet is an excellent source of information, much of it has not been verified to the degree that, say, a professional journal has been verified. Always double-check anything you find—after all, people can put anything they want on a website or blog.

Persuasive Appeals

Writers and public speakers must support their assertions with what Aristotle referred to as extrinsic or intrinsic proofs. **Extrinsic proofs** support claims with objective evidence, such as laws and confessions. **Intrinsic proofs**, also known as **artistic proofs**, are based on the speaker's character and credibility, the emotional nature of the issue, and the logic of the argument to persuade listeners.

Aristotle referred to three kinds of persuasive appeals, or intrinsic proofs, used in public speaking: logos, ethos, and pathos.

Types of Persuasive Appeals	
Logos	An appeal to reason or logic
Ethos	An appeal based on a speaker's moral character and knowledge
Pathos	An appeal to emotion

Logical proof, or **logos**, takes place when a speaker attempts to persuade an audience with rational evidence and arguments. In order for logical proof to be effective, evidence and supporting materials should connect to the arguments presented in a speech.

In modern society, **ethos** is referred to as source or speaker credibility. Credible speakers are viewed as knowledgeable about the speech topic, trustworthy, friendly, poised, believable, and energetic.

Emotional proof, or **pathos**, involves the use of emotional appeals to persuade an audience. Public speakers may evoke negative emotions from listeners, such as fear, guilt, shame, anger, and sadness. When tapping into negative emotions, the goal is to convince listeners that the proposal presented in the speech will reduce such feelings. For example, a speech aimed at convincing teenagers to stop smoking might include cancer and heart disease statistics in an attempt to arouse fear and ultimately the elimination of a harmful habit. Speeches may also arouse positive emotions, such as joy, pride, relief, hope, and compassion. A speaker who is trying to encourage the audience to volunteer with the Red Cross might describe the feelings of pride associated with assisting hurricane and tornado victims.

There are four common types of argument. One can argue from example, from analogy, from causation, and from sign. Let's look briefly at each of these.

- **Example:** Draws a conclusion from one or more instances or examples.
  - I like the paintings of Monet, Renoir, and Cassatt.
  - I like Impressionist art.
- **Analogy:** Illustrates similarities between two things or events.
  - David likes Bach, Beethoven, and Brahms. I know Kate likes Bach and Beethoven, so she will probably like Brahms. (This analogy assumes that because David likes Brahms and the others, Kate will also like all three.)

- **Causation:** Draws a conclusion that an event that occurs first is responsible for a later event.
  - Interest rates have fallen, so home sales will probably increase. (This type of logic can lead to the false-cause or *post hoc* fallacy, discussed below.)
- **Sign:** Uses an observable symptom or indicator as proof of a claim.
  - The unaffiliated candidate will be elected. She has more campaign workers and yard signs in the community.
  - I see smoke in the direction of the state park. There must be a wildfire.

Even without knowing the names of these forms of arguments, you will tend to use one or more of them in a persuasive speech. However, when arguing, be sure to avoid the common fallacies or errors that occur in public speeches, such as hasty generalizations, false-cause fallacies, invalid analogies, and ad hominem attacks. The following is a brief explanation of each.

- **Hasty generalizations** occur when a speaker uses a single event to make a generalization about a broader event or group of people, such as in stereotyping all teenagers of being rowdy based on a single negative encounter.
- **False-cause fallacies** (also known as *post hoc, ergo propter hoc* or simply *post hoc*) occur when a speaker makes the invalid assumption that one event causes another event, when in fact the events may have been coincidental. Or, as others have said more succinctly, "Correlation does not imply causation."
- **Invalid analogies** occur when a speaker compares two events or things that are in fact not alike—e.g., apples to oranges.
- **Ad hominem** refers to the fallacy of attacking (or praising) the character or integrity of the person making the argument rather than dealing with the actual issue being discussed.

ORGANIZING YOUR SPEECH

It doesn't matter how much effort you've put into research or how perceptive or logical your argument is if you end up presenting the speech in a confusing, disorganized fashion. You may have some excellent points to make, but if the speech isn't structured well, your audience will be unable to appreciate them, and will be confused—especially when you move from one point to another.

The process of organizing a speech takes time, but it's time well spent. Making the effort to organize and structure your speech will help you see which points need additional development and which ones need trimming. Organized speeches, whether they are informative or persuasive, are easier for audiences to follow and to remember. Your credibility will also be increased, because audience members are more likely to view an organized individual as competent.

Main Points

You need to organize the body of your speech even before you write the introduction or conclusion—or at least before you finalize your introduction and conclusion. After all, the process of organizing and reorganizing the body of the speech may suggest to you a different, more effective introduction or conclusion.

Use your thesis statement as a guide or starting point for developing the main points of your speech, the two to five points that will appear in the body of your speech. Why limit yourself to five main points? Because you are delivering a brief speech, not a dissertation; more points may make a speech too confusing for listeners. Keep in mind that the main parts of a speech should be:

- **Relevant and interesting:** Don't go off on a tangent, especially not a tangent that's interesting only to you.
- **Worded in a parallel style:** Parallel statements help listeners understand and follow a speech more easily than points constructed in different grammatical styles. If your first main point is phrased as an imperative—e.g., *Never go grocery shopping when hungry.*—then your remaining points should also be phrased as imperatives—e.g., *Always walk the store in a clockwise direction, because the stores expect you to walk counterclockwise and they arrange their most tempting goods so that you encounter them first.*
- **Distinct:** This means there should be no overlap among your points. If you combine points, you diminish their impact and confuse the listener. Let's look at an example. *Speed and style are the main reasons the Corvette consistently wins awards.* There are two main points given in this sentence. It's more effective to break out the points. *Speed is one of the main reasons the Corvette consistently wins awards.* Explain why that is so and then move on to your next point. *Style also plays a large role in the success of the Corvette.* Then go on to explain why that is so.

After the main points have been determined, information and supporting materials need to be structured in a strategic organizational pattern. **Strategic organization** refers to arranging a speech in a specific way in order to achieve a specific result with a specific audience. That's a large number of "specifics" at one time, but keep in mind that this is what you're trying to do; you want to tailor your speech, and the organization of that speech, to a very specific audience. That's why we refer to audience-centeredness as an important component of speechwriting.

Organizational Patterns

The best organizational pattern for a speech depends on the topic, purpose, and audience. There are six types of organizational patterns used most often in public speaking:

1. Topical
2. Temporal
3. Spatial
4. Problem-Solution
5. Cause-and-Effect
6. Motivated sequence

Topical

The **topical** pattern of speech organization is useful when a topic is easily subdivided, such as the five branches of the US military. The main points of a topical speech are parts of a whole. Topical order works well with both informational and persuasive speeches, so it is a commonly used pattern.

Temporal

With the **temporal** or **chronological** pattern of organization, the main points follow a timeline: first one thing happens, then another, and then another, and so on until the end. Temporal patterns are most often used in informative speeches. For example, a temporal pattern might be appropriate for a speech about the construction of Mount Rushmore, with the main points following the creation of the monument from the first carving until its completion. Temporal patterns are also useful when explaining a process, such as how photosynthesis works or how to change a flat tire, assemble a bicycle, or download a music file.

Spatial

Spatial order is a type of speech structure in which main points are organized in a directional pattern—top to bottom, left to right, east to west, or inside to outside. Speeches about the layout of a university or the skeletal structure of the human body would be suitable for spatial order. Spatial order is another organizational pattern that is most appropriate for informative speeches. Note that the fact that you're moving top to bottom or east to west is important; there must be a logic to your movement. You don't want to be skipping all over the place, first describing the front of the university's main office, then skipping to the basement in the chemistry lab, then jumping over to the orange grove that's part of the agriculture department, and then back to the university's main building. If it's not a spatial sequence that the listener can envision easily, they will be confused.

Problem-Solution

The **problem-solution** pattern is common in persuasive speeches when a speaker wants to convey the existence of a problem and then provide a solution that will mitigate or eliminate the problem. In this structure, the first main point focuses on the existence of the problem, and the second main point offers a solution to the problem. Keep in mind that the structure can get a bit complicated because there are often multiple problems contributing to the main one, so your solution(s) would have to address each of those.

Cause-and-Effect

Causal order, or the **cause-and-effect** pattern, organizes main points to illustrate a cause-and-effect relationship. The causal order calls for dividing a speech into two main points, similar to the problem-solution pattern. A speech about teenage drug use might be appropriate for a cause-and-effect organization. Effects of illicit drug use by adolescents would follow the potential causes. However, causal order lends itself to some flexibility—either the causes or the effects can be presented first, depending on which order is more appropriate for the topic. For example, perhaps it would be more impactful if you began your speech talking about the effects of drug use and then move into the causes. Causal order is used in both persuasive and informative speeches.

Motivated

The **motivated sequence** is an organizational pattern developed in the 1930s by Alan H. Monroe, a communications professor. Monroe created the pattern for sales presentations, but it has since been found useful in all types of persuasive and informative speeches. When you think about it, this makes perfect sense. You want to get the audience on your side, and you want them to buy into what you're saying. What better approach than something that was originally designed as a sales tool?

Motivated sequence is useful when a speaker wants listeners to respond in a positive way, so it is often employed in political speeches and advertisements. Rather than structuring a speech in three parts—introduction, body, and conclusion—as is typical of most speeches, the motivated sequence divides a speech into five steps:

1. **Step 1:** Gain attention from listeners.
2. **Step 2:** Establish a need or a problem.
3. **Step 3:** Satisfy the need by offering a solution.
4. **Step 4:** Visualize the need of being satisfied in the future.
5. **Step 5:** Ask for action from the audience to ensure the need is satisfied.

Introductions

When tasked with writing a speech, many find themselves wondering, "Where do I start?! I have no idea how to begin." If that's you, then the answer is simple: *Don't* begin. Or at least, don't begin at the beginning. You've done your research, you have some idea of the main points you want to make; don't worry yet about how to begin (or end) your speech, just start in the middle, with the body. Thinking about the points you're making will almost always provide you with that introduction (or conclusion) that you need.

Sooner or later though, you do have to come up with an introduction and conclusion, and there are many proven approaches that you can use to find a good way to begin or end your speech.

The introduction of a speech serves a number of critical functions:
- Gains the attention and interest of the audience
- Previews the topic of the speech
- Establishes speaker credibility and a connection with listeners

Speech introductions are typically about 10 percent of the entire speech, so a speech that is 500 words in length needs an introduction that is 40–60 words. Creativity is the key to a good introduction, and there are six primary types of introductions commonly used by public speakers.

Types of Introductions	
Startling statement	A shocking statement that relates to the speech topic
Rhetorical question	A question relevant to the topic that listeners answer mentally rather than vocally
Story	An interesting story related to the main point of the speech
Personal reference	An illustration of the way(s) in which the speech topic is relevant to audience members
Quotation	An attention-getting or thought-provoking quotation
Suspense	Wording that leaves the audience uncertain about the topic and raises listener curiosity

Keep in mind that introductions are only valuable if they relate directly to the speech topic. Irrelevant stories, quotations, or statements may initially intrigue listeners, but if the introduction fails to connect to the subject of the speech, listeners may become annoyed or confused. Establishing credibility and goodwill with listeners is critical during the introduction. An audience needs to perceive that a speaker is qualified to discuss a topic (i.e., that the speaker is credible) and has the best interests of listeners in mind.

Effective Conclusions

The conclusion of your speech may be the thing that leaves the most lasting impression with your listeners. Thus, good speakers take the time to construct memorable conclusions. Your conclusion should (1) alert the audience that the speech is ending, (2) summarize the speech, and (3) clarify what the listeners should think or do as a response to the speech.

There's nothing worse than an abrupt end to a speech. The audience is confused and has no idea what just happened. Is it over? Should they applaud? Wait, what was the point? It's important to provide your audience with signals that the speech is ending. Phrases such as *in conclusion* and *to summarize* are obvious cues that a speaker is preparing to stop. Experienced speakers use their voices and bodies to indicate the conclusion of a speech. Dramatic gestures, stepping away from the podium, pausing, and changing vocal pitch can also signal the end of a speech. A speaker who utilizes a **crescendo ending** builds a speech to a powerful and intense conclusion. In contrast, a **dissolve ending** evokes emotions by fading gradually to one final dramatic statement.

Summarizing your speech is your chance to recap your main points and reinforce your thesis or central idea. One way to do this is to briefly restate your main points; another way is to recast those main ideas into a single statement.

When you finish a speech, you're seeking a specific response—what's called the **anticipated response**. Especially with persuasive speeches, you want your listeners to act or think in a certain way; with informative speeches, you want your audience to *remember* certain things—what to do in case of a fire, how to reboot their computers, how to react if they happen upon a bear while on a camping trip. Your conclusion should make these anticipated responses clear to your listener, clarifying what you wish them to think or do as a result of having heard your speech. Some might phrase this as a **call to action**, and your conclusion may literally invoke such a call: *Now, don't forget, we need to show up to next week's meeting and make our views known so that we can make a positive change!*

LANGUAGE AND STYLE

The introduction, body, and conclusion of a speech are only effective if they flow well together, and the language used is appropriate for the audience. Effective public speakers address issues of language and style.

Linking with Connectives

The various elements of your speech can only flow well together if ideas are connected—i.e., linked in such a way that your listener can follow them. Linking various ideas within a speech—that is, transitioning from one idea to another—is accomplished by using words and phrases known as **connectives**. Connectives help listeners understand the relationship between one concept and another, and a speech without connectives lacks flow and confuses listeners. There are four types of connectives commonly used in public speaking: (1) transitions, (2) signposts, (3) internal previews, and (4) internal summaries.

Transitions

Transitions are words or phrases that indicate when a speaker is moving from one point to another. They are most commonly included when a speaker is shifting from the introduction to the body, from the body to the conclusion, and between main points in the speech. In the following example, the connectives are underlined.

> _Now that we have looked at_ what nanotechnology is, let's see how it is used.

Signposts

Signposts consist of brief statements that indicate to listeners where the speaker is in the speech, in the same way that signposts on a road tell you where you are on a highway. Sometimes, signposts are numerical, as in the following example:

> _The second reason_ to protect your skin with sunscreen is to prevent the development of melanoma.

Many speakers also use questions as signposts because questions invite listeners to think about the answer and become more attentive.

> So, _why do teenagers begin smoking_ when they are aware of all of these health risks?

In addition to alerting audiences to the speaker's location in a speech, signposts are also useful as a way of signaling that an important point is coming up.

> _Foremost, you need to remember that..._
>
> _Make sure that you keep this in mind..._
>
> _This is a critical point..._

Internal Previews

Internal previews are another type of connective used in the body of public speeches. As the name suggests, an internal preview is a statement that tells the audience what's coming up—that is, what to expect next. Internal previews differ from transitions and signposts because they are more detailed.

> *In discussing the effects of World War II on Japan, we'll first look at the economic consequences of the war and then at the cultural impact.*

Although internal previews are not necessary for every main point, they are useful when an audience may need assistance grasping concepts presented in a speech.

Internal Summaries

An **internal summary** is a quick review of the points that a speaker has just made. Internal summaries are especially useful when a speaker has finished discussing a complicated or especially significant point. Before moving on to the next point, the speaker will provide a statement in the form of an internal summary to remind an audience of what has just been presented.

> *As we've seen, the path leading to World War I was complex and confusing, with many seemingly random events contributing to its outbreak. But the events that followed the war were even more tumultuous.*

Effectively used connectives help speakers form coherent speeches that are easy for listeners to understand. Most speakers use a combination of different connectives to unify the main points presented in a speech.

Making the Most of Your Words

Words matter. They can be powerful and helpful or, if misused, hurtful. You know this from your interactions with friends, colleagues, and loved ones. While it's important to utilize such things as connectives in your speech to join your ideas and to help the listener move from one topic to another, those ideas will lose their impact if presented via poorly chosen, ineffective words. If you want your speech to be informative or persuasive—or both—choosing the most effective words can increase the clarity and impact of a speech. This makes vocabulary a powerful tool for the speechmaker. Your vocabulary will grow as you read and write, but there's nothing wrong with turning to a dictionary or thesaurus to find the exact word you're looking for.

Words have two kinds of meaning. The **denotative** meaning of a word is its literal and objective meaning found in a dictionary. For example, the dictionary definition of the noun *government* means "a branch of the ruling authority of a state or nation." The **connotative** meaning of a word is subjective and variable. Therefore, the connotative meaning of the word *government* includes the feelings and emotions that the word suggests— the associations your listener brings to the word, and these will vary within an audience. Some audience members may think of democracy or beneficial services that the government provides. Others may associate government with bureaucracy, politics, and overspending. Effective public speakers choose words that are less likely to set off intense reactions, and they are aware of and sensitive to a word's denotation and connotation.

> **TIP:** Be aware and educate yourself on cultural connotations. For example, in western societies, the color white is associated with purity, but in some eastern countries, white is associated with death and mourning. Not knowing this difference can have a huge impact on the effectiveness of your speech.

Using language clearly and specifically is essential to an effective speech because listeners do not have the benefit of following along with a written copy. In contrast with most written language, oral style includes the use of familiar words, connectives, and references to the speaker, such as *in my opinion* or *it seems to me*. Public speakers are also likely to use concrete words rather than abstract words. **Concrete words** refer to tangible objects that are easy to visualize, such as *flat tire, beagle,* and *digital camera*. **Abstract words**, such as *science, entertainment,* and *technology,* refer to ideas or concepts that conjure up different images for different people. Abstract words are typically more ambiguous than concrete words. Although the use of abstract words cannot (and should not) be completely avoided, speeches dominated by concrete words are typically clearer for the audience.

While concrete words serve to improve the clarity of a speech, they can also be used effectively with imagery. **Imagery** refers to vivid language included in a speech that creates mental images of experiences, objects, or concepts. Concrete words establish sights, sounds, and emotions that draw listeners into a speech, while similes and metaphors bring life and creativity to a speech. **Similes** make direct comparisons between two unlike things using *like* or *as*:

When the storm approached, the clouds swirled in the sky like cotton candy being twisted onto a stick.

The clouds aren't really cotton candy, but in some ways, they are like cotton candy. **Metaphors**, on the other hand, compare two dissimilar things without the use of *like* or *as*:

> *The air in the crowded stadium was thick with anticipation while everyone waited for the concert to begin.*

Anticipation doesn't really make air thick, but it can *feel* thick. Note the lack of the words *like* or *as*. So a combination of concrete words and vivid language (the latter often created by using metaphor and simile), can help create an effective speech.

Language used in a speech should not only be vivid and clear, but it should also be appropriate for the occasion, the audience, the topic, and the speaker. First, public speakers must adapt their language to the occasion. For example, a teacher's presentation to a small group of coworkers would be less formal than one given to the school board. Second, appropriate language avoids jargon, slang, or technical words unless the audience is familiar with such terms. Specialized vocabulary, such as medical or computer terms, is only appropriate if the audience understands it; otherwise, specialized words should be replaced with terms that are more general. Third, the speech topic also determines the appropriateness of language. A speech about how to build a birdhouse calls for straightforward language, but a speech about the art of Renoir may require imagery to convey an appreciation of his paintings. Finally, language should be appropriate to the speaker. Effective speakers convey a particular style through the language they employ. Studying the styles of other speakers may help you develop an awareness of language used in public speeches.

DELIVERING YOUR SPEECH

Most people are nervous about speaking in public. They're not as concerned with the content and organization of the speech—two aspects that we've already covered—as they are with the actual delivery. The idea of standing in front of people and delivering a speech is, for many people, frightening. Luckily, there are some tips and tricks to make it easier and, as with most things, a bit of time and practice can help you become a polished speechmaker.

TIP: Keep in mind that not everyone is the same and speakers vary in terms of how they present a speech. Techniques that work for one person may not work for another.

Types of Speeches

The following table shows the four basic methods used for speech delivery.

Methods of Speech Delivery	
Impromptu	A speech that involves little or no specific preparation
Manuscript	Entire speech is written out and read
Memorized	Entire speech is written out and memorized
Extemporaneous	Speech is prepared and presented from a basic set of notes or an outline (this is the most common method of presentation)

Impromptu Speeches

Impromptu speeches are ones that involve little or no specific preparation. Suddenly, you're simply asked (or required) to speak on a topic. This can happen in a class, but it can also happen on the job:

> *Liam, I know we haven't really had a chance to talk about this, but would you mind standing up and letting our visitors know a bit about the history of our company?*

Something similar can also happen during a job interview:

> *So, tell us about a time you failed at something, but then learned something from that failure.*

The downside to this type of speech is in its impromptu nature. Since there isn't time to research or concentrate on style and language, you must be able to think and respond based on not only your personal experience but on what you have observed of your audience. The key here is to maintain eye contact, respond to feedback, and organize your thoughts.

Manuscript Speeches

In speaking from a **manuscript**, what you're really doing is reading a speech that you've previously written out. The advantages here are that you can control the presentation time—especially useful for televised or timed speeches. Also, reading from a manuscript means that you don't need to worry about forgetting words or ideas. However, reading from a manuscript can prevent you from sounding natural (reading a speech usually sounds stilted or awkward), maintaining eye contact, and responding to audience feedback.

Memorized Speeches

As with a manuscript speech, a **memorized speech** allows you to control the timing and wording and, since you're not reading, you may be able to maintain eye contact with the audience. An obvious disadvantage is that it's possible to forget entire sections of a speech, or to flub a word or phrase and then get flustered as you try to figure out where you left off.

Extemporaneous Speeches

The extemporaneous speech is the most common method of speech delivery. An **extemporaneous speech** is researched and planned, but the precise wording of the speech is not written out. Instead, speakers refer to brief notes or an outline to remember the ideas they wish to present and the order to follow.

TIP: A set of three-by-five index cards can help. Number the cards. That way if you drop them or they get shuffled around somehow, it'll be easy to quickly restore their order.

Physical Aspects of Speech Presentation

Now that you've given some thought to the organization, content, and type of speech you're giving, it's time to consider the physical aspects of a speech: voice, articulation, and bodily movements. Since your voice conveys the words and ideas of a speech, it's important to understand the four main elements of that voice: (1) pitch, (2) volume, (3) rate, and (4) quality.

Pitch is the relative highness or lowness of your voice. People tend to speak at a pitch that's natural for them, but it's important to vary the pitch a bit in order to emphasize specific words and phrases. Doing so can help you communicate your ideas more effectively. Speaking with no variation at all results in what's known as **monotone**. The voice simply drones on and on, with no variations to set words, phrases, and ideas apart. No one wants to listen to a speaker who speaks in a monotone; there's a reason we call boring things *monotonous.*

Volume, naturally enough, refers to the loudness or intensity of the speaker's voice. Sometimes volume is a problem. A speaker's voice might fade off at the end of a sentence, or she might speak too loud. For that matter, many people habitually speak too soft.

Rate is the speed at which a person talks. Most people speak an average of about 150 words per minute; if you speak too slowly, then you lose your listeners' attention. On the other hand, if your speech is too fast, then the audience can't keep up; they will have trouble processing new information if they're still trying to sort out the information from the previous sentence.

The **quality** of someone's voice can sometimes be hard to judge since it's often a subjective measure. Nonetheless, we know that clear, pleasant tones are desirable in a public speaker. You don't want your voice to sound harsh, raspy, or nasal.

A few additional elements related to speech delivery include articulation, pronunciation, and the use of pauses. **Articulation** refers to the movement of the tongue, palate, teeth, lips, jaw, and vocal cords to produce sounds. **Pronunciation** refers to the production of syllables in a word based upon accepted standards. For example, in the word *dictionary*, articulation refers to how each of the ten letters and their sounds are shaped:

d-i-c-t-i-o-n-a-r-y

Pronunciation of the word refers to how the sounds are grouped and accented:

dik'-shuh-ner-ee

Common articulation and pronunciation problems include the following:
- **Error of Omission:** This involves leaving off a sound or a syllable in a word. A speaker may say *comp-ny* instead of *comp-a-ny.*
- **Error of Substitution:** This involves substituting one sound for another, and it may often involve substituting the letter *d* for the letter *t* or *th*. For example, the speaker will say *beder* instead of *better.*
- **Error of Addition:** Some speakers commit errors of addition by adding unnecessary sounds to words. For example, saying *ath-a-lete* instead of *ath-lete.*
- **Error of Pronunciation:** This involves accenting words incorrectly and pronouncing silent sounds. For example, emphasizing the pronunciation of the *t* in the word *often*. Linguists call this a **hypercorrection.**

Most articulation and pronunciation problems can be resolved with a bit of practice.

Pauses are a tool utilized by public speakers, but these can both help and hurt your speech. A **filled pause** is one that the speaker fills with meaningless utterances such as *ah*, *well*, and *um*. Avoid filled pauses; they make you sound tentative or unprepared. On the other hand, **brief unfilled pauses** of a second or two in length can be an effective rhetorical tool. They are appropriate at the beginning of a speech or at transitional moments as a type of connective, used to indicate that one thought has ended and that another is about to begin.

Body Language

Language is not just verbal. In addition to the words we use—and the tone we use when uttering those words—we also communicate with our bodies. **Nonverbal bodily actions**, such as eye contact, facial expressions, gestures, and movements, convey information to an audience.

By far the most important nonverbal form of communication is appropriate **eye contact** with listeners. Speakers who do not make eye contact with an audience are often perceived as aloof, uncaring, and less credible than speakers who maintain eye contact.

Facial expressions can also be effective. In addition to being universally understood, they can be used to convey emotions, including anger, fear, boredom, and excitement.

Gesturing with your hands, arms, and fingers can help emphasize points. We've all seen people who step up to a podium or lectern and then deliver a speech while standing completely still. This type of delivery comes off as wooden and stilted. It's uncomfortable for everyone, and it also tends to decrease the perceived credibility of the speaker. Instead, a good speaker uses movement of the entire body to emphasize points and to help listeners remain attentive. If the surroundings allow, a speaker can move from behind the podium, perhaps stepping to the edge of the stage or platform while addressing the audience more or less directly. This increases the connection between the speaker and the audience. It is this connection that serves to increase perceived credibility.

SUMMING IT UP

- Public speaking is one aspect of what's known more generally as **communication skills**. Knowing how to deliver a speech is not just a theoretical or intellectual exercise; it's very practical, and knowing how to speak in public will serve you well not only in your academic career, but also at work, at home, and with friends and colleagues.
- **Ethics** is the area of philosophy that concerns issues of **morality** and **fairness**. Public speakers have to make ethical choices at every stage of the speechmaking process, from selecting a topic to presenting the final message.
  - One of the most unethical public speaking actions is **plagiarism**—when writers or speakers present the ideas or words of other people as their own.
- Know your audience. The audience is your *primary* consideration when writing and delivering a speech. **Audience analysis** is the process of acquiring information about an audience in order to adapt a speech.
  - **Audience-centeredness** is making the audience the primary consideration during the entire speechmaking process.
  - **Audience identification** is the process of forming a bond with listeners by pointing out common beliefs, experiences, and goals.
- Speakers learn about listeners through **direct observation, questionnaires, demographic audience analysis**, and **situational audience analysis**.
- The three main types of speech are informative, persuasive, and entertaining.
  - An **informative** speech increases audience awareness and knowledge about a specific subject.
  - A **persuasive** speech is designed to change the attitudes, behaviors, feelings, and beliefs of listeners.
  - The purpose of an **entertaining** speech is to use humor and cleverness to amuse the audience.
- You can generate ideas for potential speech topics by:
  - **Brainstorming**
  - Checking surveys, newspapers, and magazines
  - Creating a **tree diagram** or **mind map**
  - Using the **topoi** method of asking and answering questions to generate topic ideas
- In addition to the library, the **internet** serves a significant role in modern research. While there is a wealth of information available on the internet, the accuracy of that information can be suspect because, unlike libraries, the internet lacks quality control mechanisms.

- **Research interviews** are useful for gathering information for speeches. **Follow-up questions** help gain additional information from primary questions, which are prepared in advance. **Open questions** are broad questions designed to discover an interviewee's values and perspectives, while **closed questions** tend to elicit brief answers. Always end your interview by asking your subject if they can recommend someone else to whom you can call or email.
- In a speech, **supporting material** is content that provides information, maintains listener interest, and asserts persuasive evidence. Supporting materials include examples, narratives, testimonies, and statistics.
- **Extrinsic proofs** support claims with objective evidence, such as laws and confessions. **Intrinsic** or **artistic proofs** are based on the speaker's character and credibility, the emotional nature of the issue, and the logic of the argument.
- Aristotle referred to three kinds of persuasive appeals, or intrinsic proofs, used in public speaking: **logos, ethos**, and **pathos**.
- Arguing from **example**, from **analogy**, from **causation**, and from **sign** are the common types of arguments. The four most common types of fallacies in public speeches are **hasty generalization, false cause** (also called *post hoc*), **invalid analogy**, and **ad hominem**.
- The **thesis statement** is the starting point for developing the main points of the body of a speech. Most speeches include two to five main points. Main points should be relevant and interesting to the audience and worded in a parallel format. Main points should be distinct, with no overlap among them.
- The six most common types of organizational patterns used in public speaking are **topical, temporal, spatial, problem-solution, causal**, and **motivated**.
- The **introduction** to a speech helps gain the audience's interest and preview the topic, and it establishes speaker credibility and a connection with listeners. Types of introductions include **startling statements, rhetorical questions, stories, personal references, quotations**, and **suspense**.
- The **conclusion** of a speech alerts the audience that the speech is ending, summarizes the speech, and clarifies what listeners should think or do in response to the speech.
- **Connectives** help listeners understand the relationship between one concept and another. The four most common types of connectives are **transitions, signposts, internal previews**, and **internal summaries**.
- Words have two basic kinds of meaning.
  - The **denotative** meaning of a word is its literal and objective meaning.
  - The **connotative** meaning of a word is subjective and variable, and it carries a certain amount of (positive or negative) emotional weight.

- The four basic methods of speech delivery are **impromptu, from a manuscript, from memory,** and **extemporaneous.** The latter of these is the most common.
- The **physical aspects** of speech presentation include **voice, articulation,** and **bodily movements.** Public speakers need to be aware of voice **pitch, volume, rate, quality, articulation,** and **pronunciation.**
- Common speaking errors include **errors of omission, errors of substitution, errors of addition,** and **pronunciation errors.**
- **Nonverbal bodily actions,** including **eye contact, facial expressions, gestures,** and **movements,** convey information to an audience. The most important and effective nonverbal form of communication is appropriate eye contact with listeners.

Chapter 4

Principles of Public Speaking
Post-Test

POST-TEST ANSWER SHEET

1. Ⓐ Ⓑ Ⓒ Ⓓ	16. Ⓐ Ⓑ Ⓒ Ⓓ	31. Ⓐ Ⓑ Ⓒ Ⓓ
2. Ⓐ Ⓑ Ⓒ Ⓓ	17. Ⓐ Ⓑ Ⓒ Ⓓ	32. Ⓐ Ⓑ Ⓒ Ⓓ
3. Ⓐ Ⓑ Ⓒ Ⓓ	18. Ⓐ Ⓑ Ⓒ Ⓓ	33. Ⓐ Ⓑ Ⓒ Ⓓ
4. Ⓐ Ⓑ Ⓒ Ⓓ	19. Ⓐ Ⓑ Ⓒ Ⓓ	34. Ⓐ Ⓑ Ⓒ Ⓓ
5. Ⓐ Ⓑ Ⓒ Ⓓ	20. Ⓐ Ⓑ Ⓒ Ⓓ	35. Ⓐ Ⓑ Ⓒ Ⓓ
6. Ⓐ Ⓑ Ⓒ Ⓓ	21. Ⓐ Ⓑ Ⓒ Ⓓ	36. Ⓐ Ⓑ Ⓒ Ⓓ
7. Ⓐ Ⓑ Ⓒ Ⓓ	22. Ⓐ Ⓑ Ⓒ Ⓓ	37. Ⓐ Ⓑ Ⓒ Ⓓ
8. Ⓐ Ⓑ Ⓒ Ⓓ	23. Ⓐ Ⓑ Ⓒ Ⓓ	38. Ⓐ Ⓑ Ⓒ Ⓓ
9. Ⓐ Ⓑ Ⓒ Ⓓ	24. Ⓐ Ⓑ Ⓒ Ⓓ	39. Ⓐ Ⓑ Ⓒ Ⓓ
10. Ⓐ Ⓑ Ⓒ Ⓓ	25. Ⓐ Ⓑ Ⓒ Ⓓ	40. Ⓐ Ⓑ Ⓒ Ⓓ
11. Ⓐ Ⓑ Ⓒ Ⓓ	26. Ⓐ Ⓑ Ⓒ Ⓓ	41. Ⓐ Ⓑ Ⓒ Ⓓ
12. Ⓐ Ⓑ Ⓒ Ⓓ	27. Ⓐ Ⓑ Ⓒ Ⓓ	42. Ⓐ Ⓑ Ⓒ Ⓓ
13. Ⓐ Ⓑ Ⓒ Ⓓ	28. Ⓐ Ⓑ Ⓒ Ⓓ	43. Ⓐ Ⓑ Ⓒ Ⓓ
14. Ⓐ Ⓑ Ⓒ Ⓓ	29. Ⓐ Ⓑ Ⓒ Ⓓ	44. Ⓐ Ⓑ Ⓒ Ⓓ
15. Ⓐ Ⓑ Ⓒ Ⓓ	30. Ⓐ Ⓑ Ⓒ Ⓓ	45. Ⓐ Ⓑ Ⓒ Ⓓ

46. Ⓐ Ⓑ Ⓒ Ⓓ   51. Ⓐ Ⓑ Ⓒ Ⓓ   56. Ⓐ Ⓑ Ⓒ Ⓓ

47. Ⓐ Ⓑ Ⓒ Ⓓ   52. Ⓐ Ⓑ Ⓒ Ⓓ   57. Ⓐ Ⓑ Ⓒ Ⓓ

48. Ⓐ Ⓑ Ⓒ Ⓓ   53. Ⓐ Ⓑ Ⓒ Ⓓ   58. Ⓐ Ⓑ Ⓒ Ⓓ

49. Ⓐ Ⓑ Ⓒ Ⓓ   54. Ⓐ Ⓑ Ⓒ Ⓓ   59. Ⓐ Ⓑ Ⓒ Ⓓ

50. Ⓐ Ⓑ Ⓒ Ⓓ   55. Ⓐ Ⓑ Ⓒ Ⓓ   60. Ⓐ Ⓑ Ⓒ Ⓓ

PRINCIPLES OF PUBLIC SPEAKING POST-TEST
72 minutes—60 questions

Directions: Carefully read each of the following 60 questions. Choose the best answer to each question and fill in the corresponding circle on the answer sheet. The Answer Key and Explanations can be found following this post-test.

---

1. Which of the following is NOT an element of situational analysis?

   A. Audience size

   B. Occasion

   C. Time of day

   D. Sexual orientation of the audience

2. It's not always easy to tell whether an idea is yours or whether you got it—or part of it—from another source. When in doubt, the speechwriter should

   A. cite the source.

   B. avoid using the idea.

   C. get the other person's permission.

   D. bury the reference in the middle of the speech.

3. Successful public speakers use audience analysis to adapt to audiences

   A. before a speech.

   B. after a speech.

   C. during a speech.

   D. before and during a speech.

4. Stealing from a number of sources and combining their exact words into a single speech without citing those sources is known as

   A. research.

   B. patchwork plagiarism.

   C. incremental plagiarism.

   D. global plagiarism.

5. When crafting a speech, your primary consideration should be

   A. your main topic.
   B. effective language.
   C. the purpose of your speech.
   D. your audience.

6. Aristotle's term *ethos* refers mainly to

   A. the style of the speaker.
   B. the role of the speaker as arbitrator.
   C. character of the speaker.
   D. the goal of a speech.

7. If your subject rambles when you've asked an open question, you should

   A. close down that avenue and steer the subject back to the question at hand.
   B. let them ramble, to see if interesting facts arise or if new questions come up.
   C. remind the subject of the goal(s) of the interview.
   D. turn off your recorder or stop taking notes, since this sort of thing is off the record.

8. Ethical considerations are present

   A. only in persuasive speeches.
   B. only in informative speeches.
   C. in all speeches.
   D. only in speeches delivered via mass media.

9. A tree diagram or mind map is a good tool for helping the speechwriter

   A. determine what the audience would like to hear about.
   B. focus on a narrow topic that can be addressed in a brief speech
   C. correct mistakes in logic prior to delivering the speech.
   D. judge the socioeconomic background of the audience.

10. A demographic analysis is a useful tool, but potentially dangerous because it can lead to

A. an excessively long speech.
B. awkward sentences.
C. direct observation
D. stereotyping.

11. *Topoi* is

A. the use of a question-and-answer dialog to generate possible topic ideas for a speech.
B. a method of determining whether a topic is appropriate for a specific audience.
C. a way to narrow the focus of a speech during topic selection.
D. a rhetorical device that Aristotle recommended to encourage audience interest during a speech.

12. In a persuasive speech given to an audience that is largely positive or neutral toward the topic, a thesis statement

A. should occur toward the end of the speech.
B. should occur toward the beginning of the speech.
C. is largely unnecessary since the audience already agrees with you.
D. should point out flaws in an opponent's argument.

13. During speechwriting, information gained from an audience analysis can help you

A. select a topic and examples.
B. recap or rephrase if the audience looks confused.
C. modify your volume and tone of voice.
D. adapt to audience feedback.

14. The thesis statement of an informative speech should be what sort of statement?

A. An opinion
B. Informative
C. Brief
D. Neutral

15. If the topic of the speech is an area familiar to you, then you

    A. can rely on using just stories and personal experiences from your own life.

    B. should find another topic because you are too close to this one to be objective.

    C. still need to find, evaluate, and cite additional sources for your arguments.

    D. can rely on the expertise of the speaker as your main source.

16. Which of the following is NOT a component of a demographic analysis?

    A. Age of the audience

    B. Religion

    C. Occupation

    D. Audience's view of the topic

17. Public speakers must adapt their language to the

    A. time of day.

    B. length of the speech.

    C. type of topic.

    D. formality of the occasion.

18. Which of the following is NOT a useful audience analysis tool?

    A. Direct observation

    B. Situational analysis

    C. Adaptation

    D. Questionnaires

19. Which of the following topics would make a good choice for an informative speech?

    A. Assembling a unicycle

    B. Why you should quit smoking

    C. Stop abortion now

    D. Funny stories my grandfather told me

20. If you visit a speech venue ahead of time to check out the stage, lighting, audio, etc., which of the following are you undertaking?

A. Demographic analysis
B. Situational analysis
C. Psychological analysis
D. Questionnaire-based analysis

21. If you do a good job of researching, you

A. should end up using all of your research material.
B. will always end up with extra material that you will not use.
C. will make an excellent argument in your speech.
D. will find that too much material will confuse you as you write.

22. A questionnaire is an audience analysis tool most commonly used in which of these situations?

A. A classroom speech
B. An address to a large group
C. A job interview
D. An impromptu speech

23. Which of the following is a story told to illustrate a concept or a point?

A. A narrative
B. An example
C. A set of statistics
D. An expert opinion

24. The CIA's *World Factbook* is

A. known for having a biased presentation that favors democratic governments.
B. an excellent source for information about countries around the world.
C. no longer available, having gone out of print.
D. now out of date since it's not regularly revised.

25. You might ask your interviewee an open question

    A. to elicit brief, one- or two-word answers to questions about basic facts.

    B. so that you will have time to make notes of everything the interviewee says.

    C. as a way of discovering your interviewee's values and perspectives.

    D. if you want to keep the interview strictly on topic.

26. Which of the following speech organization patterns was first developed as a model for sales presentations?

    A. Pro-and-con

    B. Cause-effect

    C. Statement of reasons

    D. Motivated sequence

27. If an example is long enough, it eventually becomes

    A. boring.

    B. a narrative.

    C. irrelevant.

    D. a testimony.

28. Which of the following would be most appropriate in a speech conclusion?

    A. Introducing a new idea

    B. Telling an old joke

    C. Listing credentials

    D. Restating the thesis

29. For some, research is the most difficult part of writing a speech, because

    A. there are few legitimate sources one can consult.

    B. it requires taking the time to find authoritative evidence to support claims.

    C. the audience can object to the sources used in the research.

    D. it requires citing the sources used in the speech.

30. Although personal testimonies can be incorporated into a speech, listeners are generally more persuaded by what sort of testimony?

A. Recent
B. Expert
C. Statistical
D. Emotional

31. An emotional proof is known as

A. logos.
B. ethos.
C. pathos.
D. credibility.

32. When examining material from the internet, you should subject it to the CRAAP test, which is used as a way to determine whether the information is

A. available for publication.
B. credible.
C. enjoyable.
D. entertaining.

33. Which of the following is a function of speech introductions?

A. Explaining your visual aids
B. Establishing your credibility
C. Summarizing the main points of your speech
D. Indicating how listeners should respond

34. Speechwriters and researchers use the CRAAP test to

A. practice their speeches in front of a mirror.
B. find out if information has already been published.
C. determine the validity of information found on the internet.
D. help evaluate the logic of their arguments.

35. A persuasive appeal based on a speaker's moral character, knowledge, and credibility is known as

A. proof.
B. ethos.
C. logos.
D. pathos.

36. If one delivers a speech that evokes strong feelings for an immoral purpose, Aristotle would have said that which of the following aspects of the speech was questionable?

    A. Logos
    B. Ethos
    C. Pathos
    D. Unity

37. Which of the following is another term for literal and objective word meanings?

    A. Connotative
    B. Emotional
    C. Denotative
    D. Imagery

38. As your interview concludes, what's the one last question you should always ask your interviewee?

    A. "Will you have time for another interview later?"
    B. "May I check with you if I have follow-up questions?"
    C. "Is there anyone else you would recommend I speak with about this topic?"
    D. "Is there anything else you would like my audience to know about you?"

39. A speech that describes a place or an object using a directional pattern would be said to be using what form of organization?

    A. Causal
    B. Temporal
    C. *Post hoc*
    D. Spatial

40. Which of the following is most likely to prove useful in determining whether your audience will respond favorably to an informative speech about modern fashion trends?

    A. Situational analysis
    B. Psychological analysis
    C. Demographic analysis
    D. Direct observation

41. If your first main point is phrased as an imperative, then your remaining points should also be phrased as imperatives. If your first point is a question, then your remaining points should also be phrased as questions. This practice is an example of what?

    A. Infinitives
    B. Parallel style
    C. Relevance
    D. Strategic organization

42. During an interview, the purpose of a follow-up question is to

    A. help gain additional information after you have asked the primary questions.
    B. throw your interviewee off-guard so that they might accidentally reveal important information.
    C. ensure that the interviewee is being truthful.
    D. gain information about the interviewee's background.

43. A speaker who develops a speech to a powerful and intense conclusion is most likely using which of the following?

    A. Motivated sequence
    B. Crescendo ending
    C. Dramatic gestures
    D. Dissolve ending

44. Transitions and signposts are examples of which of the following?

    A. References
    B. Connectives
    C. Supporting materials
    D. Calls to action

45. The topical pattern of organization is useful when the topic

    A. can be easily subdivided.
    B. occurs along a timeline.
    C. is especially controversial.
    D. is difficult to understand.

46. Which of the following is an example of plagiarism?

    A. Using and acknowledging statistics from a government agency
    B. Changing key words from a speech found in the public domain
    C. Paraphrasing information and citing the source
    D. Crediting unique ideas to the original source

47. What is one advantage of a manuscript speech?

    A. Eye contact is maintained.
    B. It's easy to respond to audience feedback.
    C. It may sound awkward or stilted.
    D. Timing can be controlled.

48. Incremental plagiarism is sometimes difficult to recognize. However, it does NOT involve

    A. stealing someone's ideas.
    B. using someone else's words verbatim.
    C. a subjective judgment.
    D. a citation in your speech.

49. The main purpose of a psychological analysis of your audience is to

    A. assure you of your listeners' sanity.
    B. find out your listeners' backgrounds.
    C. determine if your audience views your topic favorably or unfavorably.
    D. determine your listeners' political preferences.

50. An informative speech discussing the three branches of the federal government would most likely be arranged in which one of the following patterns?

    A. Temporal
    B. Topical
    C. Spatial
    D. Causal

51. A word's connotation can depend upon

    A. the tone of voice used.
    B. the denotation of the word.
    C. the culture in which the word is used.
    D. the listeners' reactions to the speech.

52. An impromptu speech is one that is

    A. delivered with little or no preparation.
    B. read from a prepared manuscript.
    C. delivered from notes or an outline.
    D. memorized.

53. A speech body that includes statements beginning with *the first cause, the second cause,* and *the third cause* is using which of the following?

    A. Supporting materials
    B. Causal order
    C. Signposts
    D. Spatial order

54. The most important nonverbal form of communication is

    A. eye contact.
    B. gestures.
    C. movement.
    D. facial expression.

55. When you evaluate support material, you seek to ensure that the information is

    A. striking and humorous.
    B. accurate and completely objective.
    C. credible and relevant.
    D. objective and entertaining.

56. Which of the following is a figure of speech that compares two unrelated things, typically with the word *like* or *as?*

    A. Metaphor
    B. Jargon
    C. Simile
    D. Gesture

57. A speaker who pronounces the *t* in *often* is exhibiting what sort of problem?

    A. Articulation
    B. Pronunciation
    C. Pauses
    D. Proxemics

58. If you were to use the phrase, "Next, we'll be talking about . . ." as a way of alerting your audience of an upcoming point, you would be using which of the following?

A. Transition
B. Signpost
C. Follow-up
D. Internal preview

59. Which of the following is the most common method of speech delivery?

A. Memorized
B. Manuscript
C. Extemporaneous
D. Impromptu

60. It's a good idea to record (or take notes during) your interview so that

A. the subject knows that they must be honest.
B. you can selectively use quotes to advance the agenda you have in mind.
C. you can be sure of getting accurate quotes and keeping your facts straight.
D. you can share your notes with others before writing the speech.

ANSWER KEY AND EXPLANATIONS

1. D	13. A	25. C	37. C	49. C
2. A	14. D	26. D	38. C	50. B
3. D	15. C	27. B	39. D	51. C
4. B	16. D	28. D	40. C	52. A
5. D	17. D	29. B	41. B	53. C
6. C	18. C	30. B	42. A	54. A
7. B	19. A	31. C	43. B	55. C
8. C	20. B	32. B	44. B	56. C
9. B	21. B	33. B	45. A	57. B
10. D	22. A	34. C	46. B	58. D
11. A	23. A	35. D	47. D	59. C
12. B	24. B	36. B	48. B	60. C

1. **The correct answer is D.** The sexual orientation of your audience may affect how you write and deliver your speech, but it is not a part of a situational analysis, which looks at the environment in which a speech is given: size of venue, size of audience, time of day, type of occasion, etc.

2. **The correct answer is A.** When in doubt, always cite the source. It's simple enough to do, so there's no need to avoid using the idea as choice B erroneously indicates. It's not always possible to get permission, so choice C is not the best answer. Including the reference in the middle of the speech without a citation (choice D) would be plagiarism.

3. **The correct answer is D.** The purpose of audience analysis is to help you adapt your speech to the specific audience. Before you give the speech, you adapt your writing to fit the audience. During the speech, you adapt to your audience in many ways, including by recapping or reviewing when you notice confusion, or by livening things up if you see that the audience is getting bored. Adapting *after* the speech (choice B) doesn't do you much good—unless you happen to be scheduled to give a similar speech to a similar audience in the near future.

4. **The correct answer is B.** Patchwork plagiarism occurs when you steal from multiple sources and use their words verbatim. Research (choice A) is how you find ideas and information,

although you must cite the sources of those ideas and that information. Incremental plagiarism (choice C) involves stealing another's ideas, while global plagiarism (choice D) is stealing large pieces (or all) of another's work verbatim.

5. **The correct answer is D.** A speech should always be crafted around the audience. Your topic, language, and purpose are certainly important, but nothing is more important than the audience—they should be your primary consideration.

6. **The correct answer is C.** *Ethos* refers to the character and credibility of the speaker, not to their style, or their role as a speaker, or to the overall goal of the speech.

7. **The correct answer is B.** The point of an open question is to *let* the subject ramble so that you can uncover new facts, come up with new questions, and find out what they think. Thus, you would never shut down (choice A) that kind of response, nor would you remind your subject of the goals of the interview (choice C). You would not stop recording or taking notes, because this type of response is *not* off the record as choice D indicates, unless you and your subject agree beforehand that it is.

8. **The correct answer is C.** Ethical considerations are always present in *all* speeches and in *all* phases of speechwriting.

9. **The correct answer is B.** A tree diagram (also known as a mind map) is an excellent tool for helping you focus on a narrow topic that you can address in a limited amount of time. The other choices are all useful things to accomplish before writing the speech, but none are specifically meant to help you narrow a topic.

10. **The correct answer is D.** A demographic analysis allows you to make assumptions about your audience based on demographic data, such as age, ethnicity, religious affiliations, etc. This can be useful, but whenever you make assumptions, you have to be careful to avoid stereotyping. This sort of analysis would normally have no effect on the length of your speech (choice A) nor on

whether it is delivered awkwardly (choice B). While direct observation can also lead to stereotyping, choice C is not the best answer because this type of analysis is not a part of demographic audience analysis.

11. **The correct answer is A.** Topoi, used by Aristotle and others as a rhetorical tool to encourage creative thinking, involves the use of a question-and-answer dialog to generate possible topic ideas for a speech.

12. **The correct answer is B.** If you're giving a speech to a group that already agrees with your main point(s), there's no reason not to state the thesis early in the speech and then go on with your examples and evidence. You might want to place the thesis statement at the end of the speech (choice A) if the audience tends to disagree with your statement, so that you can first present arguments and examples that prove your point and then follow up with the thesis statement. Choice C doesn't make sense; a thesis statement should be present in *all* speeches so that the audience can grasp the point(s) of the speech. You could very well point out flaws in an opponent's argument (choice D), but that would be done in the body of the speech, not in the thesis statement.

13. **The correct answer is A.** While writing your speech, your analysis of the audience can guide you as you select a topic and also as you choose examples to use to illustrate that topic. The other three options are indeed adaptations you might want to make, but they would be made during the delivery of the speech, not as it was being written.

14. **The correct answer is D.** A thesis statement for an informative speech should be neutral. You're not writing a persuasive speech, so there's really no place for an opinion (choice A) in the thesis statement. While the body of the speech will be informative, choice B is incorrect because the thesis statement need not be. Similarly, a thesis statement could indeed be brief (choice C), but there's nothing that says it absolutely has to be.

15. **The correct answer is C.** Being familiar with the topic of the speech is definitely an advantage, for you can use life stories and personal experiences as supplementary supporting material. However, don't rely too much on personal experiences or stories, as choice A suggests. You will still need to do your research, to find material that will further support your personal experiences and overcome any unintentional biases in your objectivity. If you support your speech with additional sources, you won't need to find another topic as choice B suggests. Choice D doesn't make sense, because you are the speaker in this case. In addition, it's not good practice to rely solely on the expertise of a single source for a speech. Effective supporting material for any speech comes from multiple, credible sources.

16. **The correct answer is D.** A demographic analysis includes such things as age, gender, religion, sexual orientation, ethnicity, economic status, occupation, education, and organizational membership. It does not include the audience's view of your topic, which is a component of a psychological analysis, not a demographic one.

17. **The correct answer is D.** The formality of the occasion has a great effect on the language used by the speaker. Neither of time of day (choice A) nor the length of the speech (choice B) would affect the speaker's choice of language. The type of topic (choice C) should have little effect on the language used; the topic could be something formal or something lighthearted, but it is the formality of the occasion that should have the greatest effect.

18. **The correct answer is C.** Adaptation is the *purpose* of the analysis, not an audience analysis tool. Direct observation (choice A), situational analysis (choice B), and questionnaires (choice D) are all tools used to analyze an audience.

19. **The correct answer is A.** There could certainly be an informational element to all of these, but the only one whose purpose is purely informational—that is, explanatory— is the one about assembling a unicycle. "How to" speeches are almost always primarily informative, as are speeches that explain how a process works. Choices B and C would be appropriate for persuasive

speeches, and telling funny stories (choice D) might be a good approach if you were writing a speech meant to be amusing.

20. **The correct answer is B.** A situational analysis is an examination of the environment in which the speech will be given; it includes everything from time of day to lighting, and from the size of the venue to the type of audio equipment used. A demographic analysis (choice A) seeks to understand your listeners' backgrounds and values, while a psychological analysis (choice C) is aimed at determining whether the audience views your topic favorably or unfavorably. Questionnaires (choice D) can be very effective, but their use is limited, and that sort of tool would have nothing to do with visiting the setting of a speech beforehand.

21. **The correct answer is B.** If you're doing a thorough job of researching, you'll generally end up with too much information. Choice A is incorrect because some of the information will remain unused but that's okay because having too much information allows you to pick and choose the best, most convincing evidence and ignore the rest. Conversely, if you skimp on the research, you are likely to have trouble with the writing and then end up going back to do more research. It's better to do all of the legwork ahead of time. Doing good research is no guarantee that your argument will be strong (choice C); that depends on how well you use that research and how effectively you write the speech. While you could confuse yourself with too much information, choice D is not the best answer because this confusion would more likely be due to a poor or faulty thesis statement, or poor organization of your research results.

22. **The correct answer is A.** A questionnaire is an excellent audience analysis tool to use when preparing for a classroom speech. Your fellow students could answer it at home and send (or bring) in their answers, and the group is small enough to make analyzing their answers feasible. It would be difficult to use a questionnaire with a large group (choice B), and in a job interview (choice C) or impromptu speech (choice D). In these situations, you would have no time to prepare (and get responses to) a questionnaire.

23. **The correct answer is A.** While an example, a set of statistics, and an expert opinion all serve to illustrate a concept or a point, only a narrative is by definition a story.

24. **The correct answer is B.** The *World Factbook* is an extensive work that lists facts about places around the world. It does not display any biases as choice A indicates. The book is strictly an objective listing of information, including population, location, economy, and other data about just about every country in the world. Choice C is incorrect because the *World Factbook* is still available in print, though it's more accessible (and less expensive) to view online. The *World Factbook* is not out of date as choice D erroneously indicates. The book is quite current. In fact, one advantage of publishing it on the internet is that it's easy to update.

25. **The correct answer is C.** The point of an open question is to allow your subject to ramble a bit, to talk about their thoughts, values, and ideas. It's definitely not a way to elicit brief answers (choice A) or to ensure that you'll have time to take notes (choice B). You should be taking notes regardless. If you wanted to keep the interview strictly on topic (choice D), ask a few closed questions.

26. **The correct answer is D.** Alan Monroe developed the motivated sequence pattern as a technique for giving sales presentations. Since then, the pattern has been used in political speeches and advertisements. None of the other methods presented were developed for sales presentations. The pro-and-con (choice A) and the cause-effect (choice B) speech organization patterns are both useful for informative and persuasive speeches. The statement of reasons pattern (choice C) is used in persuasive speeches and recommends that you place the weakest reason in the middle of your list of reasons, the second-strongest first, and your strongest reason last, so that it leaves the biggest impression.

27. **The correct answer is B.** An example, if it's long enough, eventually becomes a story of its own—that is, a narrative. It need not be boring (choice A), even if it's long, and it may not become irrelevant (choice C). A testimony (choice D) is an opinion.

28. **The correct answer is D.** Restating the thesis, or central idea, of the speech is appropriate in a conclusion because it reminds the audience about the specific purpose of the presentation. Introducing a new idea (choice A) is a common mistake because the focus of the conclusion should be on concepts already developed in the speech. Telling a joke (choice B) is inappropriate for most speech conclusions, and speaker credentials (choice C) should be established during the introduction.

29. **The correct answer is B.** If you're giving a speech that requires evidence (and most do), then you'll need to take the time and make the effort to find that evidence and ensure that it's legitimate. Choice A is not true. There are actually many legitimate sources available, though it can take some time and effort to locate and assess them. The audience is unlikely to object to your sources as choice C indicates, especially if you've done a good job of researching your topic. Citing your sources within the speech (choice D) is neither difficult nor time-consuming.

30. **The correct answer is B.** The most effective form of testimony is that given by experts in the field being discussed. It's more important for testimony to be a relevant opinion of someone regarded as an expert, rather than recent (choice A). Statistics (choice C) are good, when used in moderation, but they're not a form of testimony. An emotional opinion (choice D) may be useful, but what's important is that the opinion, emotional or not, comes from an expert.

31. **The correct answer is C.** Pathos is an appeal to emotion, and it could evoke either positive or negative emotion in order to make its point. Logos (choice A) is an appeal to logic, while ethos (choice B) is an appeal to credibility. Credibility itself (choice D) is a sought-after attribute but is not itself a type of emotional proof.

32. **The correct answer is B.** You need to determine that the information you wish to use is credible—that is, believable and accurate. It's already been published (choice A), and you can legally use portions of it as long as you cite the source. It doesn't really matter whether the material is enjoyable (choice C) or entertaining (choice D).

33. **The correct answer is B.** Establishing speaker credibility is one of the primary functions of a speech introduction. Visual aids (choice A) may be used in an introduction to gain listener attention but explaining them is not the purpose of an introduction. Summarizing the main points of your speech (choice C) and indicating how listeners should respond (choice D) are functions best left to the conclusion of a speech.

34. **The correct answer is C.** The CRAAP test is used to determine the validity and accuracy of information found on the internet. The test has nothing to do with practicing speeches (choice A), finding out whether the information has been published (choice B), or evaluating logic (choice D).

35. **The correct answer is B.** An appeal based on the speaker's character is known as ethos. Choice A is not the best answer because all persuasive appeals are known as *intrinsic proofs*. Logos (choice C) and pathos (choice D) are, respectively, appeals to logic and emotion.

36. **The correct answer is B.** Ethos refers to the character and credibility of the speaker. If the goals of the speech were immoral, Aristotle would have said that the character and credibility of the speaker were questionable. Logos (choice A) refers to logic, while pathos (choice C) refers to emotion. Unity (choice D) is not something with which Aristotle dealt with in this context.

37. **The correct answer is C.** Denotative meanings are those that are literal and objective; these are the meanings found in the dictionary. Connotative meanings (choice A) are those suggested by word associations. Emotional meanings (choice B) would be the same as connotative, given that there is an emotional association, whether positive or negative. Imagery (choice D) is vivid language that creates word images for an audience.

38. **The correct answer is C.** These are all excellent questions to ask your subject near the end of the interview, but the very last thing you should ask is whether your interviewee can recommend another person as a source of information.

39. **The correct answer is D.** A directional pattern (north, west; up, down; forward, back) is known as spatial. It is useful for describing places and objects in an organized, understandable fashion. Causal (choice A) and temporal (choice B) are other organizational patterns. A *post hoc* argument (choice C) is a logical fallacy, not an organizational pattern.

40. **The correct answer is C.** A demographic analysis lets you learn about listeners based on things such as age, gender, religion, sexual orientation, ethnicity, etc. These are likely to tell you whether the audience would be interested in fashion trends. A situational analysis (choice A) would tell you about the environment in which you'll be delivering the speech, but it wouldn't tell you anything about the listeners' preferences. A psychological analysis (choice B) is generally used to determine whether the audience views your topic favorably or unfavorably, but that analysis is normally used when preparing for a persuasive speech. Direct observation (choice D) might be a tempting answer, since you might assume that you could gauge your listeners' interest in fashion by what they are wearing, but that might not always be true.

41. **The correct answer is B.** Using the same phrasal structure as you make each main point is known as *parallelism*. Parallel statements help listeners understand and follow a speech more easily than points constructed in different grammatical styles. You might choose to use infinitives (choice A), but that doesn't necessarily imply parallelism. Neither relevance (choice C) nor strategic organization (choice D) has anything to do with using parallel grammatical structures.

42. **The correct answer is A.** The point of a follow-up is to gain additional information related to a primary question. In most interviews, there is no need to attempt to throw your subject off-guard (choice B) or to ensure that they are being truthful (choice C). If you are using a follow-up to ask about your subject's background (choice D), then your interviewing technique is weak, because asking about their background should be a primary question.

43. **The correct answer is B.** A crescendo ending is characterized by building toward a powerful and intense conclusion. A motivated sequence (choice A) is a type of persuasive pattern. Some speakers use dramatic gestures to signal conclusions. However, choice C is not the best answer because those gestures might accompany a crescendo ending, and it would be the crescendo ending itself that is more powerful. A dissolve ending (choice D) is emotional, but it fades gradually to a dramatic statement.

44. **The correct answer is B.** Connectives are words and phrases that link ideas in speeches. Transitions and signposts are types of connectives. References (choice A) and supporting materials (choice C) support ideas but do not connect them. A call to action (choice D) is presented in the conclusion and is intended to invoke a response from the audience.

45. **The correct answer is A.** A topical pattern is used when dividing your speech into main parts that align with the parts of the subject being discussed. For example, the five branches of the service, eight systems that make up an automobile, the three types of motorcycle helmets, etc. This way, the main points of your speech can correspond with the main parts of a whole. Choice B describes a temporal pattern. Choices C and D are incorrect because the subject may or may not be especially controversial or difficult to understand.

46. **The correct answer is B.** Changing key words from a speech found in the public domain is an example of plagiarism. Even though the material is in the public domain, that doesn't mean you can use it without giving credit. Nor can you simply change a few words and call it your own work. The other choices are all ethical ways to use the material.

47. **The correct answer is D.** With a manuscript speech, it's easy to control the timing, because you can deliver the exact same speech during practice until you get the timing where you want it; if you need a speech of exactly four minutes, you can write and practice it so that it takes exactly that long to deliver. Eye contact (choice A) is very desirable, and the inability to maintain eye contact is a disadvantage of reading from a manuscript. Similarly, it's very

difficult to respond to feedback (choice B) when reading a speech. The fact that it may sound awkward (choice C) is a disadvantage of reading a speech from a prepared manuscript.

48. **The correct answer is B.** Incremental plagiarism involves the use of someone else's ideas, rather than their actual words. It is sometimes subjective, and it does require that you cite in your speech the source of the ideas.

49. **The correct answer is C.** A psychological analysis is used to determine how willing your audience is to listen to the speaker. Generally, this comes down to whether they're knowledgeable about the subject and whether they view the topic in a favorable or unfavorable light. In spite of the name, the analysis doesn't actually tell you anything about the listeners' sanity (choice A), nor does it address their backgrounds (choice B). A psychological analysis normally wouldn't tell you about the audience's political preferences (choice D).

50. **The correct answer is B.** Topical patterns are useful for speeches in which the topic is easily subdivided, so in this case, each main point would address one branch of the government. Choices A, C, and D are useful patterns for other types of speeches, but less appropriate for a speech describing parts of a whole.

51. **The correct answer is C.** Connotative meanings (positive or negative associations with the word) are the associations your listeners bring to the word. These are emotional associations, and a word's connotative meaning can depend on the culture in which the word is used. For example, not all cultures view the color white as a symbol of purity and the color black as a symbol of evil. Choice A is not the best answer because while the tone of voice could have an impact on the current connotation, past associations would heavily influence the current connotation. The denotation of the word (choice B) is the dictionary meaning, which is the opposite of connotation. Choice D is not the best answer because while the listeners may react to the use of a word, that reaction would not affect the word's connotations.

52. **The correct answer is A.** An impromptu speech is one that is delivered with little or no warning or preparation. You're given a subject and required to deliver a speech right then and there. Speaking from a manuscript (choice B) involves reading a speech you've previously written out. Delivering a speech from notes (choice C) is known as extemporaneous speech, while one you've memorized (choice D) is simply known as speaking from memory.

53. **The correct answer is C.** Signposts are connectives that help audiences keep track of points in a speech. Supporting materials (choice A) are materials that help prove a point. Choices B and D refer to organizational patterns used in speeches, not to types of connectives. Supporting materials are the examples, narratives, and statistics included in a speech.

54. **The correct answer is A.** Eye contact is the most important and most effective form of body language for a speaker. Gestures (choice B), movement (choice C), and facial expressions (choice D) are important aspects of nonverbal communication, but none are as effective as appropriate eye contact.

55. **The correct answer is C.** You need to make sure that your material is credible and relevant. The information should be striking or unique (choice A), but it need not be humorous. While it should be accurate, it need not be completely objective (choice B); after all, you may be using an opinion piece as support material— any facts it contains should be credible, but the piece is not likely to be completely objective. The material may not be at all entertaining (choice D), and that's okay.

56. **The correct answer is C.** A comparison that uses the words *like* or *as* is called a simile. A metaphor (choice A) is a comparison that does not use *like* or *as*. Jargon (choice B) is specialized, technical language—sometimes referred to as "shop talk." A gesture (choice D) is a nonverbal communication involving movement of the hands.

57. The correct answer is B. Pronouncing an unpronounced letter in a word is a pronunciation problem. A typical articulation problem (choice A) might be adding a sound where one does not belong. Filled and unfilled pauses (choice C) are typical of many speeches but do not involve adding sounds to words. Proxemics (choice D) refers to how space is used by a speaker during a presentation.

58. The correct answer is D. An internal preview alerts the audience about the next main point to be presented. Transitional words or phrases (choice A) are connectives that help a speaker move from one point to another, but they do not indicate the subject of the next point. Signposts (choice B) tell listeners where a speaker is in a speech and do not indicate the next point. A follow-up (choice C) is a type of question that occurs in response to an interviewee's answer to a previous question.

59. The correct answer is C. An extemporaneous speech is the most common type of speech delivery; it tends to allow eye contact as well as response to feedback, and if you lose your place, you can glance at your notes or outline. A memorized speech (choice A) may let you maintain eye contact and control the timing, but it's easy to get flustered and lose your place or forget parts of the speech. A manuscript speech (choice B) is read to the audience, which can sound awkward and stilted. An impromptu speech (choice D) is delivered with little or no preparation; this is fairly common in speech or debate classes, or on the job, but rare elsewhere.

60. The correct answer is C. Recording your interview is a way to help make sure that your facts, recollections, and quotes are accurate. We assume that the subject knows enough to be honest (choice A), and if they were dishonest, taking notes would probably not change that. You should never selectively use quotes out of context (choice B) in order to advance your own agenda, and there's normally no need to share your notes with others (choice D), unless this happens to be a group project.

Like what you see? Get unlimited access to Peterson's full catalog of DSST practice tests, instructional videos, flashcards, and more at **www.petersons.com/testprep/dsst.**

9 780768 944709